CHARMING
SMALL HOTEL
GUIDES

SPAIN

Including: MAJORCA, MINORCA, IBIZA, FORMENTERA

1992

CW00549626

CHARMING
SMALL HOTEL
GUIDES
SPAIN

Including: MAJORCA, MINORCA,
IBIZA, FORMENTERA

1992

Edited by Chris Gill

DUNCAN PETERSEN

This edition published 1992 by
Duncan Petersen Publishing Ltd,
54 Milson Road, London W14 0LB,
and distributed by
AA Publishing, Exel Logistics DMS,
Invicta Warehouse, Sir Thomas Langley Road,
Medway City Estate, Rochester, Kent

Conceived, designed and produced by Duncan Petersen
Edited by Fox + Partners, The Old Forge,
Norton St Philip, Bath BA3 6LW

Editor Chris Gill
Assistant editors Julia Letts, Amanda Crook
Principal inspectors Nick Inman, Clara Villanueva, Hilary Hughes, Stuart Morris
Proof reader Joshua Dubin
Art director Mel Petersen

A CIP catalogue record for this book is available from the British Library

ISBN 1 872576 12 5

Typeset by Fox + Partners, Bath,
and PCS Typesetting, Frome
Originated by Reprocolor International S.R.I., Milan
Printed by G. Canale & C. SpA, Turin

Contents

Introduction

This guide to Spanish hotels is a new addition to the *Charming Small Hotel Guides* – a series already covering France, Italy and the British Isles. The guides are different from other accommodation guides on the market. They are designed to satisfy what we believe to be the real needs of today's traveller; needs which have been served at best haphazardly by other guides.

The most fundamental difference is suggested by the title: we aim to include only those hotels and guest-houses which are in some way captivating, and which are small enough to offer truly personal service, usually from the owner. In Spain, where hotels with hundreds of rooms are common, most of our recommendations have fewer than 40 rooms, and only a few have more than 60.

The guides are different in other ways, too: their descriptive style is different, and they are compiled differently. Our entries employ, above all, words: they contain not one symbol. They are written by people with something to say, not a bureaucracy which has long since lost the ability to distinguish the praiseworthy from the mediocre. The editorial team is small and highly experienced at assessing and writing about hotels, at noticing all-important details. Every entry, however brief, aims to give a coherent and definite feel of what it is actually like to stay in that place.

Although we have made use of reports from members of the public, and would welcome more of them (see box following this introduction) we have placed great emphasis on consistency in our selections and our descriptions.

These are features which will reveal their worth only as you use your *Charming Small Hotel Guide*. Its other advantages are more obvious: it contains colour photographs of practically all the entries; and it simplifies the job of finding a hotel to suit your needs – the entries are presented in clear geographical groups, and each entry is categorized by the type of accommodation (for example, country inn or seaside hotel).

Spanish hotels, large and small
Small hotels have always had the special appeal that they can offer the traveller a personal welcome and personal attention, whereas larger places are necessarily more institutional. In Spain, this distinction is particularly valid.

The establishments described in this guide are simply the 200 or so hotels, guest-houses, inns and bed-and-breakfast places that we believe most discriminating travellers would prefer to stay in, given the choice. About 160 hotels are described in detail, in full entries of a page or half a page; the remainder are covered in two other

Introduction

ways. First, in each major regional section there is a feature box devoted to the Paradores of that region; Paradores are a uniquely Spanish institution, described in detail later in this introduction. Secondly, for some areas where we are conscious that there are many hotels other than our entries that a traveller might like to know about, we have included an area introduction summarising some of those hotels.

Our ideal hotel has a peaceful, pretty setting; the building itself is either handsome or historic, or at least has a distinct character. The rooms are spacious, but on a human scale – not grand or intimidating. The decorations and furnishings are harmonious, comfortable and impeccably maintained, and include antique pieces that are meant to be used, not revered. The proprietors and staff are dedicated, thoughtful and sensitive in their pursuit of their guests' happiness – friendly and welcoming without being intrusive. Last but not least, the food, whether simple or ambitious, is fresh, interesting and carefully prepared. Elaborate facilities such as saunas or trouser-presses count for little in these guides, though we do generally list them.

Of course, not every hotel included here scores top marks on each of these counts. And, to be frank, we have been disappointed by the standards of Spanish hotels compared with those of France, Italy and the British Isles; in Spain, hotels that approach our ideal are few, and far between. The buildings Spanish hotels occupy are often splendid, and all the hotels listed here are at least adequately run; but you rarely encounter the really excellent family-run hotel which has long been such an essential element of the hotel scene in France and Italy, and is now evident in the British Isles. Nevertheless, we are confident that staying in any of the hotels recommended here will enrich any trip through Spain – and our descriptions make clear which ones are the happy exceptions to the rule.

Going to Spain

We are pleased to acknowledge the assistance, in preparing this guide, of the U.K. tour operator Magic of Spain and the U.K. airline GB Airways. Magic of Spain operates a large and varied programme of holidays, featuring many of the hotels in the guide. Tel 081- 748 4659 (brochures); 081- 748 7575 (reservations). Our inspectors travelled to southern Spain on GB Airways' regular scheduled flights (using modern Boeing jets) from London Gatwick to Jerez de la Frontera. Tel (0293) 664239.

Introduction

Paradores

The state-run chain of Paradores dominates the Spanish hotel scene just as many of the castles the hotels occupy dominate the surrounding landscape. They are not the best hotels in Spain, and few of them are notably good by absolute standards – though in any given locality the Parador is quite likely to be the best in town, for the simple reason that many have been created in areas which private enterprise might not find attractive. But Paradores do have great attractions: many are set in wonderfully atmospheric old buildings – mansions, convents, hunting lodges as well as magnificent castles – and many others have spectacular mountain settings. Others are simply very convenient for the traveller on the road, being strategically positioned to fill gaps on the map of Spain.

In terms of their qualities as places to stay, Paradores are much less impressive. Their strong point, usually, is the bedrooms, which are normally very spacious and well furnished. Public rooms may be comfortable and inviting, but may equally be dismally furnished and gloomy. Food, which aims to reflect regional traditions, may be highly satisfactory or extremely ordinary. Service is equally unpredictable, and seems to depend more on individual initiative than any management policy.

Parador room prices vary widely (unlike meal prices, which are almost uniform). In the tourist Mecca of Granada, for example, you pay over twice what you pay in remote mountain areas – around 16,000pts for a double room, rather than 7,000pts; in most established tourist haunts – Toledo, Córdoba or Santillana del Mar, say – you pay something between these extremes, often around 12,000pts.

Are they worth these prices? For most people, we judge that the answer is a qualified yes. The best of the Paradores – which you will be able to identify from our descriptions and photographs – really can add something to your travels. But we would not recommend planning a trip entirely around Paradores; not only would the cost mount up alarmingly, but the drawbacks of these somewhat inconsistent establishments might begin to weigh more heavily, while the special appeal that they have might begin to pall.

In our entries, we have abbreviated the proper name Parador Nacional to the letters PN.

Introduction

Reporting to the guide

The *Charming Small Hotel Guides* are greatly strengthened by reports from people who have stayed in the hotels recommended in them, or who have found other places which seem to deserve an entry. Particularly helpful reporters earn a free copy of the next edition of the guide concerned. On page 11 is further information about reporting to the guide.

How to find an entry

In this guide, the entries are arranged by province, and the provinces are clustered in convenient regional groups. The regions, and within them the provinces, are arranged in a sequence starting in the extreme north-west (La Coruña) and working west to east and north to south. The Balearic Islands (Majorca and its neighbours) come last in the sequence.

To find a hotel in a particular area, simply browse through headings at the top of the pages until you find that area – or use the maps following this introduction to locate the appropriate pages. To locate a specific hotel or a hotel in a specific place, use the indexes at the back, which lists the entries alphabetically, first by name and then by place-name.

How to read an entry

At the top of each entry is a coloured bar highlighting the name of the town or village where the establishment is located, along with a categorization which gives some clue to its character. These categories are, as far as possible, self-explanatory.

The letters PN in the name of a hotel stand for Parador Nacional (see explanatory box earlier in this Introduction).

Fact boxes

The fact box given for each hotel follows a standard pattern which requires little explanation; but:

Under **Tel** we give the telephone number starting with the area code used within the country; when dialling from another country, omit the initial 9 of this code.

Under **Location** we give information on the setting of the hotel and on its car parking arrangements, as well as pointers to help you find it.

Under **Food & drink** we list the meals available.

Under **Prices** we normally give the range of prices you can

Introduction

expect to pay for a room, including tax and service – from the cost of the cheapest single room in low season to the cost of the dearest double in high season. Wherever possible we have given prices for 1992, but for many hotels these were not available when the guide was revised in late 1991. Prices may therefore be higher in 1992 than those quoted, simply because of inflation. But bear in mind also that the proprietors of hotels and guest-houses may change their prices from one year to another by much more than the rate of inflation. Always check before making a booking.

After the room price, we normally give the prices of breakfast and other meals. If room-only or bed-and-breakfast terms are not available, we give either the price for dinner, bed and breakfast (DB&B), or for full board (FB) – that is, all meals included.

Under **Rooms** we summarize the number and style of bedrooms available. Our lists of facilities in bedrooms cover only mechanical gadgets, and not ornaments such as flowers or consumables such as toiletries or free drinks.

Under **Facilities** we list public rooms and then outdoor and sporting facilities which are either part of the hotel or immediately on hand; facilities in the vicinity of the hotel but not directly connected with it (for example, a nearby golf course) are not listed here, though they sometimes feature at the end of the main description in the Nearby section, which presents a selection of interesting things to see or do in the locality.

We use the following abbreviations for **Credit cards**:
  AE American Express
  DC Diners Club
  MC MasterCard (Access/Eurocard)
  V Visa (Barclaycard/Bank Americard/Carte Bleue etc)

The final entry in a fact box is normally the name of the proprietor(s); but where the hotel is run by a manager we give his or her name instead.

Hotel prices in Barcelona are likely to be much increased during the 1992 Olympic Games, 25th July to 9th August; and in Seville during Expo '92, 20th April to 12th October.

Reporting to the guides

Please write and tell us about your experiences of small hotels, guest-houses and inns, whether good or bad, whether listed in this edition or not. As well as hotels in Spain, we are interested in hotels in Britain and Ireland, Italy, France, Portugal, Austria, Switzerland, Germany and other European conntries, and those in the eastern United States.

The address to write to is:

Chris Gill,
Editor,
Charming Small Hotel Guides,
The Old Forge,
Norton St Philip,
Bath, BA3 6LW,
England.

Checklist
Please use a separate sheet of paper for each report; include your name, address and telephone number on each report.

Your reports will be received with particular pleasure if they are typed, and if they are organized under the following headings:

Name of establishment
Town or village it is in, or nearest
Full address, including post code
Telephone number
Time and duration of visit
The building and setting
The public rooms
The bedrooms and bathrooms
Physical comfort (chairs, beds, heat, light, hot water)
Standards of maintenance and housekeeping
Atmosphere, welcome and service
Food
Value for money

We assume that in writing you have no objections to your views being published unpaid, either verbatim or in an edited version. Names of major outside contributors are acknowledged, at the editor's discretion, in the guide.

If you would be interested in looking at hotels on a professional basis on behalf of the guides, please include on a separate sheet a short CV and a summary of your travel and hotel-going experience.

Hotel location maps

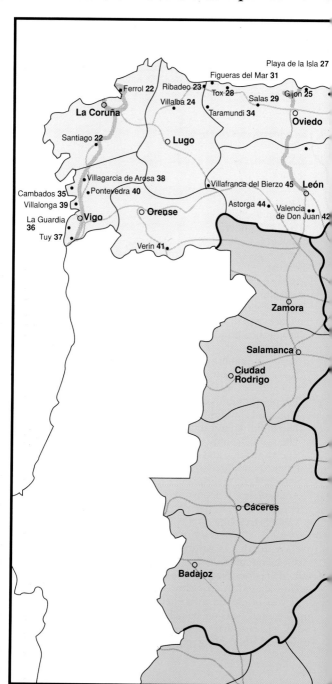

Hotel location maps

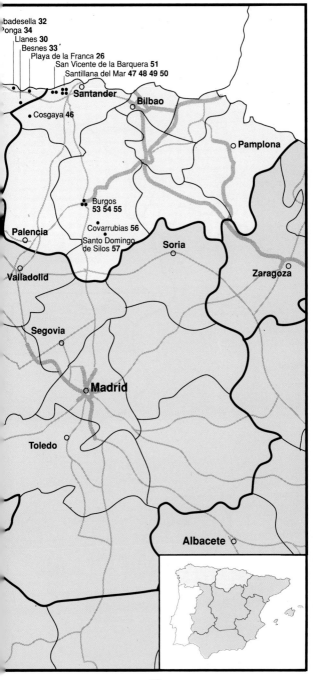

badesella **32**
Ponga **34**
Llanes **30**
Besnes **33**
Playa de la Franca **26**
San Vicente de la Barquera **51**
Santillana del Mar **47 48 49 50**

Santander

Bilbao

Cosgaya **46**

Pamplona

Burgos
53 54 55

Palencia

Covarrubias **56**
Santo Domingo
de Silos **57**

Soria

Valladolid

Zaragoza

Segovia

Madrid

Toledo

Albacete

Hotel location maps

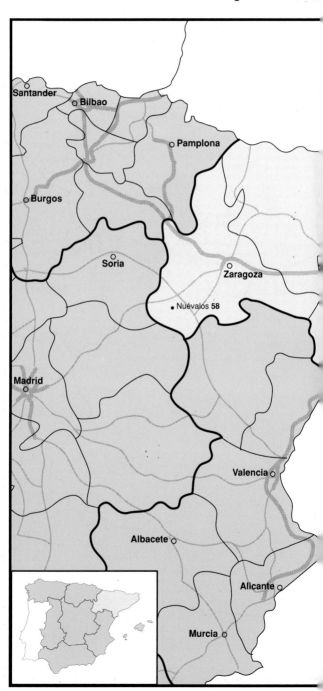

Hotel location maps

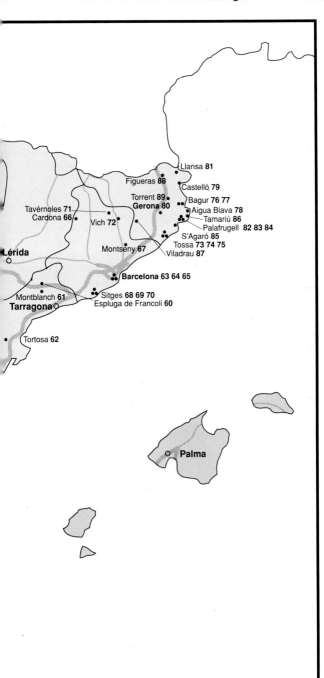

Llansa **81**

Figueras **88**

Castelló **79**

Torrent **89**
Gerona 80

Bagur **76 77**

Aigua Blava **78**

Tamariú **86**

Palafrugell **82 83 84**

Tavérnoles **71**
Cardona **66**

Vich **72**

S'Agaró **85**

Montseny **67**

Tossa **73 74 75**

Viladrau **87**

Lérida

Barcelona 63 64 65

Montblanch **61**

Sitges **68 69 70**

Tarragona

Espluga de Francoli **60**

Tortosa **62**

Palma

15

Hotel location maps

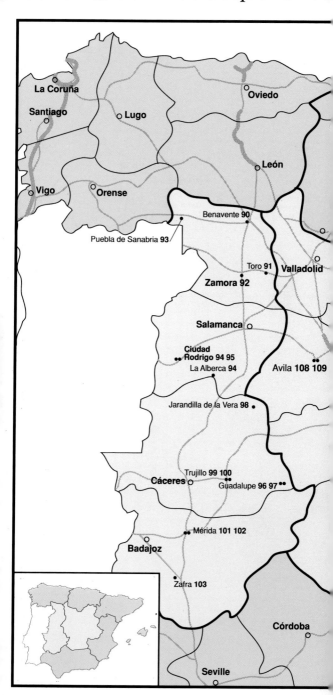

Hotel location maps

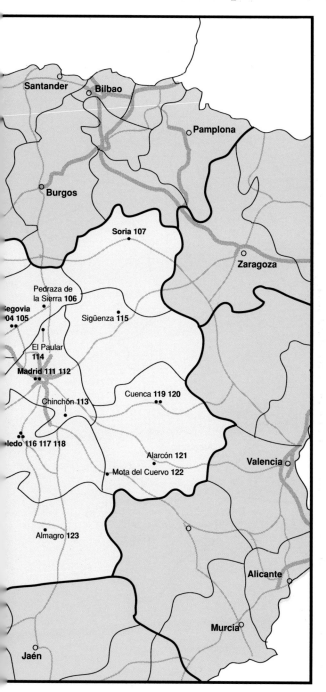

Santander
Bilbao
Pamplona
Burgos
Soria 107
Zaragoza
Pedraza de
la Sierra 106
Segovia
104 105
Sigüenza 115
El Paular
114
Madrid 111 112
Cuenca 119 120
Chinchón 113
Toledo 116 117 118
Alarcón 121
Valencia
Mota del Cuervo 122
Almagro 123
Alicante
Murcia
Jaén

Hotel location maps

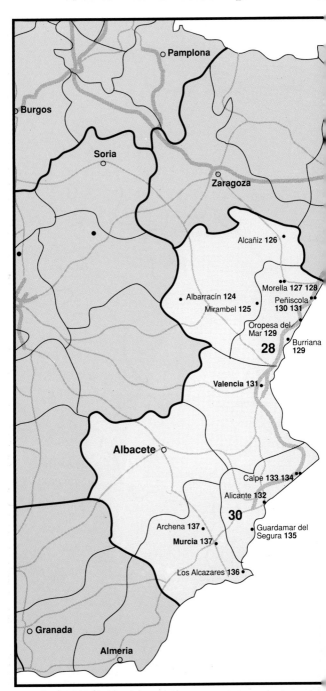

- Pamplona
- Burgos
- Soria
- Zaragoza
- Alcañiz **126**
- Morella **127 128**
- Albarracín **124**
- Peñiscola **130 131**
- Mirambel **125**
- Oropesa del Mar **129**
- **28**
- Burriana **129**
- Valencia **131**
- Albacete
- Calpe **133 134**
- Alicante **132**
- **30**
- Archena **137**
- Guardamar del Segura **135**
- Murcia **137**
- Los Alcazares **136**
- Granada
- Almeria

Hotel location maps

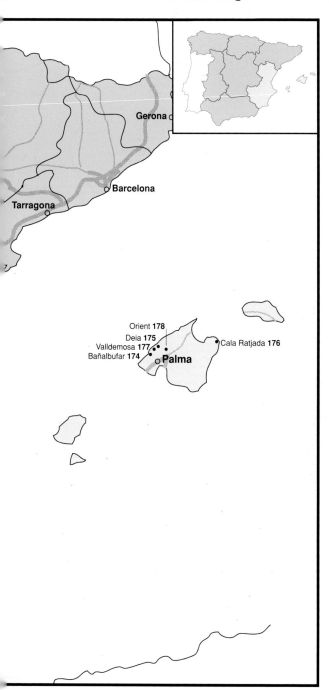

Gerona

Barcelona

Tarragona

Orient **178**
Deia **175**
Valldemosa **177**
Bañalbufar **174**
Palma
Cala Ratjada **176**

Hotel location maps

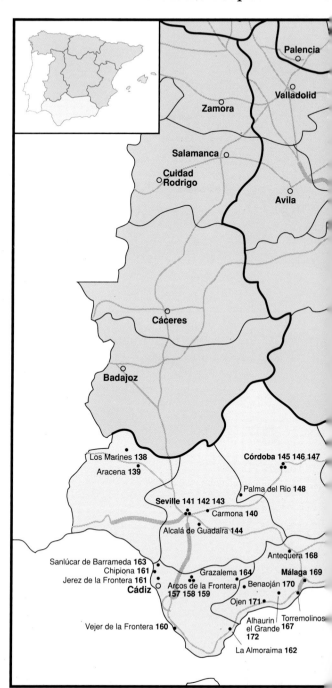

Palencia

Valladolid

Zamora

Salamanca

Cuidad Rodrigo

Avila

Cáceres

Badajoz

Los Marines **138**

Aracena **139**

Córdoba 145 146 147

Palma del Rio **148**

Seville 141 142 143

Carmona **140**

Alcalá de Guadaira **144**

Antequera **168**

Sanlúcar de Barrameda **163**

Chipiona **161**

Jerez de la Frontera **161**

Cádiz

Grazalema **164**

Málaga 169

Arcos de la Frontera **157 158 159**

Benaoján **170**

Ojen **171**

Vejer de la Frontera **160**

Alhaurin el Grande **172**

Torremolinos **167**

La Almoraima **162**

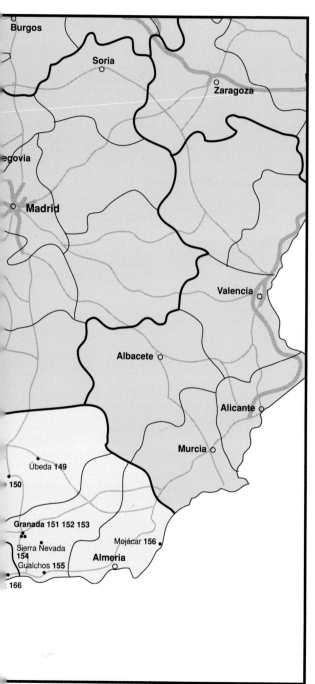

La Coruña

La Estela

Santiago, with its relics of St James, has attracted pilgrims for centuries, and today people come for the beautifully preserved old city with its cathedral, squares and museums. This tiny, family-run *hostal* is tucked away in a corner right opposite one of Spain's most grand and opulent hotels (Los Reyes Católicos, now part of the Parador chain) – a rather interesting contrast, particularly if you compare prices. There is no restaurant here but the surrounding streets are packed with places to eat. The rooms are very basic but they are clean and quite adequate for a night's stop.

Nearby Cathedral, Old Town and the Hospital Real.

Rajoy No 1, 15700, Santiago de Compostela, La Coruña
Tel (981) 582796
Location in heart of old town, by Parador and cathedral; no private car parking
Meals breakfast
Prices rooms 3,000-3,500pts; breakfast 150pts
Rooms 14 double, all with bath; all rooms have central heating

Facilities breakfast room
Credit cards not accepted
Children welcome
Disabled no special facilities
Pets not accepted
Closed never
Manager Eduardo Pedrido Fontao

PN de Ferrol

This is a distinctly nautical Parador, standing above the main dockyards of the Spanish 'Armada' and beside the barracks of the Marines: there is a huge anchor in the car park, the sitting-room is lined with tapestries and paintings of ships and sea battles, and the lamps are brass and hang from chains. The sea even makes itself felt in the restaurant with an interesting smoked fish salad with fruit, tuna steaks or sea bream.

The cobbled streets of the old town of Ferrol are worth exploring, but use your feet or the one-way system will probably defeat you.

Nearby Visits to naval dockyards; Caaveiro Monastery (20 km).

Plaza Eduardo Pondal, 15400, Ferrol, La Coruña
Tel (981) 356720
Location in square overlooking port and dockyard; with garage and car parking in square
Meals breakfast, lunch, dinner
Prices rooms 8,500-9,500pts; breakfast 1,100pts, dinner 3,200pts
Rooms 28 double, 11 single, all with bath; all rooms have central heating, air-conditioning, phone, TV, minibar
Facilities dining-room, sitting-room, bar
Credit cards AE, DC, MC, V
Children welcome
Disabled access difficult
Pets not accepted
Closed never
Manager Enrique Matas Torres

Lugo

Modern Parador, Ribadeo

PN de Ribadeo

Ribadeo is now reached by an elegant road bridge which spans the mouth of the *ria* effectively bypassing the more picturesque towns of Figueras and Castropol which used to lie en route. The Parador finds itself in a quiet backwater of the town since the change in the traffic flow, but it is only a short walk into the town centre.

The building itself is nothing special and parts of it are showing their age. It overlooks the harbour which has the usual array of fishing boats, from one-man ventures to larger deep sea vessels, all bringing their catches right to the door. There is also a mineral-loading quay which can make clouds of dust if the wind is blowing the wrong way. The restaurant here, as you would expect, has an interesting selection of fish on the menu – also soups, salads, *hors d'oeuvres*, grills and stews.

The atmosphere here is informal, friendly and relaxed while offering all the more home-like Parador standards. One comment from a guest was surprise at the lack of spoken English on the reception desk, particularly as so many British use this hotel on their way to and from Galicia via Santander.

Nearby Early Romanesque Church of San Martín de Mondoñedo, near Foz (23 km); Los Castros beach (5 km).

Amador Fernández, 27700, Ribadeo, Lugo
Tel (982) 110825
Location above harbour in quiet part of town; with garden, garage and car parking
Meals breakfast, lunch, dinner
Prices rooms 8,000-15,500pts; breakfast 1,100pts, dinner 3,200pts
Rooms 41 double, all with bath; 6 single, 5 with bath, one with shower; all rooms have central heating, phone, TV, minibar
Facilities dining-room, sitting-room, 2 other sitting-areas, bar
Credit cards AE, DC, MC, V
Children welcome
Disabled access easy; 2 ground-floor rooms
Pets not accepted
Closed never
Manager Eligio Dominguez

Lugo

Historic Parador, Villalba

PN Condes de Villalba

This is one of the smallest and most interesting of the Paradores. There are only six rooms, so it is as well to book ahead, particularly in the busiest summer months.

The octagonal tower of Los Andrade stands high above the little town of Villalba, surrounded by the old cobbled streets and squares of the original village, looking out over pleasant rolling countryside. Ask for the key to the roof area for a fabulous all-round view.

The walls of the building are something over six feet thick, and the only window to your room will probably be a tiny arrow slit, so even the all-night celebrations of midsummer, with street parties, fireworks and bonfires, will not keep you awake. In the morning the screeching of swifts and the cheeping of sparrows will be the only sounds to reach you when you open your shutters.

The dining-room is in the cellars, down a grand staircase, with a huge fireplace, wrought iron chandeliers and the atmosphere of a baronial hall, even though it is not huge. The wines and food reflect the produce of the area with, for once, a generous selection of salads and fresh fruit.

Nearby Lugo (36 km), the ancient walled provincial capital.

Valeriano Valdesuso, 27800, Villalba, Lugo
Tel (982) 510011
Location in heart of old part of town, with garden; parking for 5 cars
Meals breakfast, lunch, dinner
Prices rooms 11,000-12,000pts; breakfast 1,100pts; lunch and dinner 3,200pts
Rooms 6 double, all with bath; all rooms have central heating, phone, TV, minibar
Facilities dining-room, lobby
Credit cards AE, DC, MC, V
Children accepted
Disabled lift/elevator
Pets not accepted
Closed Dec
Manager José Vázquez Cámara

Asturias

Modern Parador, Gijón

PN El Molino Viejo

Gijón is huge and hot, and has an extremely complicated one-way system – though some of the residential areas and the coastal stretch are attractive. The Parador is by the Parque Isabel la Católica, beside the massive new stadium. It is loosely based around an old watermill, though there is little evidence of this today – the leat runs through the courtyard into the lake in the park. The hotel itself is a haven of peace, and is one of the more stylish of the Paradores, attracting local business people to the restaurant and bar. The bedrooms are elegant, and many overlook the park.

Nearby fishermen's quarter, Santa Catalina.

Parque Isabel la Católica,
33203, Gijón, Asturias
Tel (98) 5370511
Location by stadium in quiet park; with garden and car parking
Meals breakfast, lunch, dinner
Prices rooms 11,000-12,000pts; breakfast 1,000pts; dinner 3,200pts
Rooms 39 double, 1 single, all with bath; all rooms have

central heating,
air-conditioning, phone, TV, minibar, radio, hairdrier
Facilities 2 dining-rooms, sitting-room, bar
Credit cards AE, DC, MC, V
Children accepted
Disabled ground-floor rooms; lift/elevator
Pets not accepted
Closed never
Manager Angel Montero

Paradores in North-west Spain

North-west Spain has more than its fair share of Paradores – and many of these are small and charming enough to have earned detailed entries . The province of Pontevedra (bordering Portugal on the west coast) is particularly well endowed, with four Paradores within a hundred kilometres of one another. The largest of these (124 rooms), the PN Conde de Gondomar at Bayona, is a smart modern hotel built within the walls of an ancient fortress. It has all the classic ingredients – crenellated walls, pillared balconies, an open courtyard, richly decorated rooms, beautifully manicured lawns and spectacular views of the Ría de Vigo (Tel (986) 355000). By local standards Bayona is expensive, but it does not even come close to the Reyes Católicos in Santiago de Compostela – one of the most expensive Paradores, but also one of the most superior and most historic, built in the 15th century to house pilgrims from all over Europe who came to pay homage at the shrine of St James in Santiago's magnificent cathedral (Tel (981) 582200). Beware 25th July: this is the feast day of St James, and the city (and Parador) are packed.

Léon's central 253-room Parador, San Marcos, notable for its fabulous façade and two-storey cloisters and once a watering-hole on the pilgrim route to Santiago, is now a smart hotel, laden with antiques and surrounded by formal gardens (Tel (987) 237300).

Asturias

Seaside hotel, Playa de la Franca

Hotel Mirador de la Franca

At the mouth of a small river, the beach of La Franca is relatively small at high tide, providing a safe anchorage for small boats in the stream bed. But when the tide goes out a huge expanse of sand provides ample play space for everyone, including residents of the large campsite behind the hotel.

The Mirador is built on the eastern side overlooking the bay, with its steep cliffs and savagely rocky headlands. From outside the building looks modern and unexciting, but inside the decoration and changes in level make the hotel pleasantly home-like, comfortable and interesting without being fussy or elaborate. There is plenty of wood panelling, stone and tiling about, softened by rugs and comfortable chairs. Many of the bedrooms and the restaurant look out over the constantly changing sea and, as at every restaurant along this coast, there is an interesting selection of fresh fish and shellfish on the menu.

All in all, a satisfactory base for a few days, especially for a family. There is no town of any size immediately at hand but there are plenty of holiday facilities at the hotel itself, and it is no distance to the mountains.

Nearby Cueva del Pindal (5 km) – prehistoric paintings and engravings.

33590, La Franca, Asturias
Tel (98) 5412145
Location next to La Franca beach, E of La Franca, 20 km W of San Vicente de la Barquera; with car parking and campsite behind hotel
Meals breakfast, lunch, dinner
Prices rooms 3,700-7,900pts; breakfast 500pts; meals 1,400pts
Rooms 63 double, all with bath and shower; all rooms have central heating, phone,

TV
Facilities dining-room, sitting-room, bar; tennis, table-tennis, minigolf
Credit cards AE, DC, MC, V
Children welcome; play area
Disabled access difficult
Pets not accepted
Closed restaurant only, 18 Sep to 14 Jun
Manager Felipe Sordo Tomas

Asturias

Seaside hotel, Playa de la Isla

Hotel Bahía

The sheltered beach of La Isla has no harbour for fishing boats so the people here are farmers, and the village is known for the number and size of its *horreos*, or granaries. Several large old private villas suggest that the attractions of the beach have been recognized for some time; but, remarkably, it has escaped exploitation. Three years ago Aurora Artidello realized here her dream of opening her own hotel, and with her husband Joe, home from a lifetime at sea (with perfect English), she has created a welcoming holiday retreat.

The building is new but low and unobtrusive, simply furnished, and decorated with Joe's paintings. All the bedrooms, the bar and restaurant look out over the bay, and part of the terrace is under cover, with comfortable cushioned cane chairs where you can enjoy your breakfast or pre-dinner drink. There is a constant menu of *platos combinados* and a daily dinner menu specially for guests which is freshly cooked and good value, with plenty of salads and interesting local dishes.

Despite the modest nature and scale of the place, Aurora does not compromise on the housekeeping; towels are changed daily, for example.

Nearby Mirador del Fito (15 km) – stupendous views .

Playa de la Isla, Asturias
Tel (98) 5857032
Location on unspoilt beach about 18km W of Ribadasella; with parking for about 15 cars
Meals breakfast, lunch, dinner
Prices rooms 4,200-6,000pts; breakfast 350pts; meals 1,700pts
Rooms 10 double, all with bath; all rooms have central heating
Facilities dining/sitting-room, cafeteria, terrace
Credit cards not accepted
Children welcome
Disabled some ground-floor rooms
Pets not accepted
Closed Oct to Mar
Proprietor Aurora Artidello

Asturias

Country hotel, Tox

Villa Borinquen

This delightful hotel could not be more secluded – even the village of Tox does not appear on most maps (look for Villapedre). Between the main coast road and the shore, the Villa Borinquen sits quietly, unsignposted, amid rolling green cultivated land, far from any distractions.

It is a modern building, based on the houses of the wealthy Spaniards who returned from the Americas in the heyday of Spanish colonialism, and everything has been put together with comfort in mind. The bedrooms are enormous, and some have huge balconies overlooking the countryside and the extensive gardens to the sea. They are all carefully and individually furnished with large beds, comfortable armchairs, long drapes at the windows and rugs on the polished wood floors.

The hotel provides breakfast and snack meals, and the same management runs a restaurant down the road at the pretty little village of Puerto Vega, which has something of the atmosphere of a Cornish fishing village. Fish and shellfish are unloaded straight into the kitchen; you can watch the harbour at work as you eat and take a stroll along the sea wall as the sun goes down.

Nearby Barayo beach (5 km); the dramatic Navia valley (10 km).

Tox, , Villapedre, Asturias
Tel (98) 5648220
Location in open fields near village, 1 km N of N634, about 11 km W of Luarca; with grounds and car parking
Meals breakfast
Prices rooms 6,500-10,000pts with breakfast
Rooms 8 double, 3 family rooms, all with bath; all rooms have central heating, phone, TV, minibar, hairdrier

Facilities sitting-room, breakfast room, bar
Credit cards MC, V
Children welcome; games available
Disabled access easy; lift/elevator
Pets not accepted
Closed never
Manager Manuel José Pérez

Asturias

Historic town hotel, Salas

Castillo de Valdés-Salas

The market town of Salas is off the busy and tortuously winding road between Oviedo and the coast, in the foothills of the Cordillera Cantabrica. The town's 16thC castle has recently been restored and converted into a small and simple hotel, keeping much of the character of the original building intact

The massive doors lead you through the thick walls into the reception area, which also houses the local tourist information desk (both offering good spoken English). The building is constructed around a paved courtyard, with covered cloisters to shelter you from the mountain rain and from the summer sun. On the ground floor, off this patio area, is the cafeteria/restaurant, whch is open to the public and serves unfussy dishes with local touches – try their cakes made with rice, milk and sugar, served with freshly brewed coffee. The bedrooms are mostly on the first floor and are very plain but stylish, with shutters at the windows, wooden floors and modern bathrooms tiled in red and white. There are two sitting-rooms upstairs; one has a television, games and books, and both have open fires in the winter. All the windows are double-glazed too, so it should be snug.

Nearby Benedictine monastery of San Salvador, Cornellana (10 km); viewpoint at Tineo (24 km).

Plaza General Aranda, 33860, Salas, Asturias
Tel (98) 5831037
Location in village just off N634, about 45 km W of Oviedo; with garden and car parking in square
Meals breakfast, lunch, dinner
Prices rooms 5,899pts; breakfast 600pts; meals 800pts
Rooms 12 double, 5 with bath, 7 with shower; all rooms have central heating, phone

Facilities dining-room, 2 sitting-rooms, bar, terrace
Credit cards AE, MC, V
Children accepted
Disabled access difficult
Pets not accepted
Closed never
Proprietor Manuel López Espiña

Asturias

Town hotel, Llanes

Hotel Don Paco

The most startling feature of this hotel is the restaurant, which occupies the huge arched and vaulted hall of the original 17thC palace that forms the basis of the present-day building. It is truly impressive, with stone pilasters, an ancient polished wood floor and splendid chandeliers, and a mezzanine area from where you can survey the other diners. Local specialities include a spiny lobster which is caught in pots off the coast. Double doors lead out on to the terrace which is above the level of the pavement, beneath pollarded plane trees and shrubs sheltering the tables from the sun and the passers-by. From here you can admire the handsome stone façade of the palace as you take your coffee or aperitif.

The rest of the the hotel is rather dull in comparison, and showing signs of wear, but many of the old-fashioned bedrooms look out over the quiet square or the back of the building away from the traffic. The town itself is full of bustle and interesting shops, as well as the remains of its defensive walls and castle. There are plenty of beaches nearby and the grand Picos de Europa with their rivers and mountains are within easy reach.

Nearby Monasterio de S. Antolin (10 km); Pena Tu (5 km) – megalith with engravings.

Posada Herrera 1, 33500, Llanes, Asturias **Tel** (985) 400150 **Location** in heart of town; with some car parking **Meals** breakfast, lunch, dinner **Prices** rooms 7,150; breakfast 500pts; meals 1,750pts **Rooms** 38 double, 36 with bath, 2 with shower; 4 single with shower; all rooms have central heating, phone, TV **Facilities** dining-room,	sitting-room, bar **Credit cards** AE, DC, MC, V **Children** accepted **Disabled** lift/elevator; some ground-floor rooms **Pets** not accepted **Closed** never **Manager** Alfredo Sanpedro Concha

Asturias

Town hotel, Figueras del Mar

Palacete Peñalba

This extraordinary house was build in 1912 by a disciple of the celebrated Spanish architect Antonio Gaudí. Everything about it – the curved sweep of the entrance steps, the ovals of the balconies, the glazed and tiled atrium, the twin towers with their delicate plasterwork, the arched alcoves in the bedrooms – is redolent of the early Art Nouveau movement which took root in Europe at this time. Much of the original furniture and internal decoration, such as the tapestries, has been preserved, and the whole edifice has been declared a National Artistic Monument. In fact, the atmosphere does rather resemble that of a museum – beware the elegant but delicate chairs in the sitting-room. This is not a place to bring unruly children, but if you enjoy the absurdities of this particular era you will come anyway.

The town of Figueras del Mar has been by-passed by the new bridge over the Ria de Ribadeo, but it is busy with fishing and shipbuilding. The hotel's owners also run a restaurant on the waterfront, and both establishments have a reputation in the area for interesting cuisine – specializing, needless to say, in seafood.

Nearby Castropol (5 km); beach and lighthouse at Tapia de Casariego (10 km).

33794, Figueras, Asturias
Tel (98) 5623150
Location at top of town above port; with grounds and car parking
Meals breakfast, dinner
Prices rooms 8,000-10,000pts; breakfast 550pts; dinner 2,200pts
Rooms 12 double, 2 suites, all with bath; all rooms have central heating, radio, TV
Facilities dining-room, sitting-room
Credit cards AE, DC, MC, V
Children welcome
Disabled access difficult
Pets not accepted
Closed never
Proprietor Adeuna Guitierrez

Asturias

Seaside hotel, Ribadesella

Hotel Ribadesella Playa

Ribadesella has long been quite a stylish resort, popular with holiday-makers attracted by the port and the estuary of the river Sella, with its sandy beaches and spectacular scenery. The Hotel Ribadesella Playa, converted from one of the many old family villas which line the bay, across the river from the main town, has recently been sensitively modernized.

The hotel is right on the beach, beside a grassed promenade, free of traffic, and many of the bedrooms – smartly done up with traditional-style modern furniture – have long windows and balconies with views over the water. The restaurant is in the lower part of the house, cool and airy, with stone floors and sympathetic wooden furniture. The *carte* is long and varied, with plenty of fresh fish dishes, and there is also a menu of the day if you prefer your selection made for you.

The hotel has no pretensions to luxury, but combines comfortable accommodation with a relaxed and informal atmosphere. A happy choice for a beach holiday, with the added advantage for many visitors of the nearby town and the mountains with their walks, caves and birdlife.

Nearby Caves of Tito Bustillo (5 km); Mirador de la Reina (45 km).

Paseo de la Playa, 33560, Ribadesella, Asturias
Tel (98) 5860715
Location in quiet residential beach area on W side of town; car parking in courtyard
Meals breakfast, lunch, dinner
Prices rooms 4,000-6,900pts; breakfast 400pts; meals 1,600pts
Rooms 4 double, all with bath; all rooms have central heating, phone, TV

Facilities dining-room, 2 sitting-rooms
Credit cards AE, DC, MC, V
Children accepted
Disabled no special facilities
Pets not accepted
Closed never
Manager José Luis García

Asturias

Mountain hotel, Besnes

La Tahona

Driving from Panes up into the Picos de Europa, you follow the course of the Rio Cares, up through a deep and dramatic gorge which winds on towards some of the most stupendous views to be found in these mountains. La Tahona is tucked away behind the tiny village of Besnes, at the end of a cobbled track, beside a stream which runs down through beech woods – a peaceful and simple base for walking, riding or mountain-biking (or, in winter, cross-country skiing). This is one of several attractive country hotels developed (or at least marketed) by the government of Asturias under the name Rural Tourism Centres.

The bar by the entrance hall is used by a few local farmers who drop in for a quiet coffee and brandy on their way up and down the valley; beyond is the rustic restaurant, all bare stone, logs, whitewashed rough plaster and red tiles. Bedrooms are similarly simple but stylish, with tiled or wooden floors.

The stream runs past the restaurant, the terrace and the windows of the bedrooms – the sound of water and birdsong will be your only distractions while contemplating the choice between salmon with cider, trout from the river or Asturian hotpot. **Nearby** El Buxu – prehistoric cave paintings (30 km); viewpoint at Las Estazadas (8 km).

33578, Besnes-Alles, Asturias
Tel (98) 5414249
Location in quiet wooded valley, off C6312 10 km W of Panes; with garden and car parking
Meals breakfast, lunch, dinner
Prices rooms 4,950-6,900pts; breakfast 450pts; meals 1,500pts
Rooms 18 double, one family room, all with bath; all rooms have central heating, TV

Facilities dining-room, sitting-room; horse-riding, mountain bikes, fishing
Credit cards MC, V
Children welcome; play-room; special menus
Disabled access easy; some ground-floor rooms
Pets not accepted
Closed never
Manager Fernando Castano Tricas

Asturias

Mountain hotel, Ponga

La Casona de Mestas

To reach this mountain hideaway you follow the sinuous course of the Ponga river to the regional capital of San Juan de Beleño, passing below sheer rocky hillsides and climbing over beautiful passes. The hotel – another Rural Tourism Centre – is at the heart of some of the most spectacular walking country you could hope to find anywhere, with several well known routes starting at the Casona itself. The main building has been converted from an old house with overhanging, Alpine-style roofs, and the restaurant area is a sympathetic modern, wooden glass-sided extension looking out on to fabulous views of the surrounding peaks.

Nearby Desfiladero de los Beyos (25 km).

33557, Ponga, Asturias
Tel (98) 5843055
Location in mountainous countryside near village, about 30 km S of Cangas de Onis; with car parking
Meals breakfast, lunch, dinner
Prices rooms 4,900-6,100pts; breakfast 500pts; meals 1,500pts
Rooms 14 double, all with bath; all rooms have central heating
Facilities dining-room, cafeteria, TV room
Credit cards V
Children accepted
Disabled no special facilities
Pets not accepted
Closed one month in winter
Manager Vicente Cosío

Mountain hotel, Taramundi

La Rectoral

This was the first of the Rural Tourism hotels to be encouraged by the government of Asturias – a lovely old 18thC stone house converted into simple but comfortable accommodation reflecting the architectural, decorative and gastronomic traditions of the region. It is on the western side of Asturias, on the border with Lugo, in the remote hilly country of Los Oscos. The Rectoral looks out over unspoiled countryside which is still quietly tilled using locally made tools. Six of the bedrooms have their own lounge and private terrace, sharing the peaceful view with the hotel's patio.

Nearby Monastery, Villanueva de Oscos (20 km).

33775, Taramundi, Asturias
Tel (98) 5634060
Location on hill, on western fringe of Asturias, about 25 km SW of Vegadeo; with car parking
Meals breakfast, lunch, dinner
Prices rooms 8,900-11,200pts; breakfast 750pts; meals 1,750pts
Rooms 12 double, all with bath; all rooms have central heating, air-conditioning, phone, TV, radio, minibar
Facilities dining-room, sitting-rooms, TV room, cafeteria, sauna, gymnasium
Credit cards AE, DC, MC, V
Children accepted
Disabled no special facilities
Pets not accepted
Closed never
Manager Jesus Manuel Mier

Pontevedra

Mansion Parador, Cambados

PN del Albariño

Cambados is a happy little holiday town which is at its best in the summer months, a judgement equally applicable to the Parador, which can be bleak and cold in winter (like any hotel in an abandoned seaside town in the off-season).

The hotel is built around a courtyard garden with palm trees and a fountain, and for anyone in vacation mood it offers cool and relaxed accommodation, right beside the protected estuary of the Ría de Arousa, with its islands and wooded banks. The water here is not as clean as Atlantic water would be, but this does not seem to deter local bathers.

There are several interesting bars and restaurants in the town with its peaceful, shady squares and long tree-lined promenade if you decide not to eat in the rather predictable Parador dining-room. Inevitably the specialities of this area are fish and shellfish, but most menus offer meat dishes too. The wines of the west coast can be delicious, particularly some of the young green wines, known locally as *joven* – the Parador itself is named after a wine brought to the area by Benedictine monks in the twelfth century.

Nearby Plaza de Fefiñanes; Monastery of Armenteira (10 km); island of La Toja (10 km).

Paseo de Cervantes, 36630, Cambados, Pontevedra
Tel (986) 542250
Location in lovely gardens at north end of promenade; with car parking
Meals breakfast, lunch, dinner
Prices rooms 8,800-10,000pts; breakfast 1,100pts, dinner 3,200pts
Rooms 51 double, 12 single, all with bath; all rooms have central heating, phone, TV

Facilities dining-room, sitting-room, bar
Credit cards AE, DC, MC, V
Children welcome
Disabled some ground-floor rooms
Pets not accepted
Closed never
Manager Carlos Herrero Soler

Pontevedra

Restaurant with rooms, La Guardia

Hostal Fidelmar

South of Bayona the coast becomes steep and rocky with little respite from the battering Atlantic Ocean. Every now and again there is a tiny bay, and this little family-run *hostal* occupies one of them. The sandy beach is no more than 100 m long, protected by arms of rock reaching out into the sea, and on a sunny evening it will be alive with local youngsters.

The *hostal* is behind the beach, across the single track road, and is very basic with white-painted rooms, shutters and white muslin curtains. But there is plenty of hot water to wash away the salt and the sand, there is nothing to keep you awake but the sound of the sea, and the restaurant, La Perla del Caribe, is just along the beach.

Señor Alvarez, his wife and daughter, are masters of the art of understanding dim-witted foreigners, and bring you freshly cooked regional specialities and a local wine which is good, but not too expensive. Try their hake baked with potatoes and tomatoes or, at lunchtime, a mouthwatering array of home-prepared *tapas*. But be quick, they are already talking excitedly about building a big hotel...

Nearby Monte de Santa Tecla (5 km); Monterreal, Bayona (35 km).

Calle José Antonio 38, 32540,
La Guardia, Pontevedra
Tel (988) 610008
Location on old coast road
near beach; car parking
around back of beach
Meals breakfast, lunch, dinner
Prices rooms (1991) 4,000pts;
no meal prices available
Rooms 10 double, all with
bath and shower
Facilities dining-room, bar
Credit cards MC, V

Children accepted
Disabled access difficult
Pets not accepted
Closed 30 Sep to 1 Jun
Proprietor Manuel Vicente
Alvarez Fidel

Pontevedra

Modern Parador, Tuy

PN San Telmo

Tuy has been one of the major crossing points into Portugal since the bridge across the Miño was built in 1884. If you need a place to recuperate after a long hot drive, this Parador fits the bill – set on a pleasantly green and breezy hilltop overlooking the river.

The building itself was designed to mirror the style of large country houses in the region and consequently it is simple and airy with doors opening from the dining-room on to the shady terrace with its views of the town, countryside and Portugal across the water. Many of the bedrooms (well up to normal Parador standards) also have balconies with heavy wooden shutters. The gardens are prettily laid out on the steeply sloping grounds and include a fair-sized swimming-pool and a tennis court.

Tuy is, on first sight, busy and uninteresting, but the narrow stepped streets of the old town, topped by the cathedral, are worth exploring. This area is known for its hot springs and you can take a thermal bath at the extraordinary old spa in Caldelas, five kilometers upriver. This is also hunting and fishing country, so you may find salmon and game on the menu in season.

Nearby Santo Domingo Gardens; Miño valley.

36700, Tuy, Pontevedra
Tel (986) 600309
Location above bend in Miño river, overlooking Portugal; with shaded car parking
Meals breakfast, lunch, dinner
Prices rooms 7,000-10,000pts; breakfast 1,100pts, lunch and dinner 3,200pts
Rooms 20 double, one single, one suite, all with bath; all rooms have central heating, phone, TV

Facilities dining-room, sitting-room, bar; swimming-pool, tennis court
Credit cards AE, DC, MC, V
Children accepted
Disabled some ground-floor rooms
Pets not accepted
Closed never
Manager Amando Baños

Pontevedra

Country hotel, Villagarcía de Arosa

Hotel Pazo O'Rial

The road here runs along beside the Ría de Arosa as it opens out towards the sea, not quite the open Atlantic, but nevertheless a holiday area for many Spanish visitors as well as northern Europeans.

This lovely old manor house is set back from the coast in its own gardens and has been beautifully converted, making full use of all the usual traditional effects – wooden beams, tiled floors and bare stone walls. The whole effect is softened with deep cushioned sofas, lacy curtains and woollen rugs. The service has been criticised as slack (and certainly the desk clerk was rather slow) but there is nothing amiss with the housekeeping, the gardening or the cleanliness of the pool, which is surrounded by a protective hedge on one side and lovely views over the countryside on the other.

This is another area famous for its seafood – the bays around here are packed with fish and shellfish farms, and every inlet seems to have its little fleet of fishing boats to win a share of the harvest. The menu of the hotel reflects this, with the ubiquitous grilled prawns coming high on the list along with huge mussels in a thick tomato sauce.

Nearby Vista Alegre Convent; Mirador de Lobeira (5 km).

El Rial No 1, 36600,
Villagarcía de Arosa,
Pontevedra
Tel (986) 507011
Location near sea, set back
from road; with car parking
Meals breakfast, lunch, dinner
Prices rooms 7,000-13,500pts;
breakfast 600pts
Rooms 56 double, 4 suites, all
with bath; all rooms have
central heating, phone, TV
Facilities dining-room,

sitting-room, bar
Credit cards AE, DC, MC, V
Children welcome
Disabled access easy;
ground-floor rooms;
lift/elevator
Pets not accepted
Closed never
Manager Julio Mondragon

Pontevedra

Country hotel, Villalonga

Hotel Pazo El Revel

Back from the coast road and the small town of Villalonga, up a lane which leads to walks in the hills, a little church and the local cemetery, this lovely 17thC *pazo* is the family home of Luis Ansorena Garret, an aristocratic gentleman who has run this hotel along his own lines for the last 25 years.

The creeper-covered façade has no noticeboard or sign to give the hotel away. You park across the lane and help will be at hand to carry your bags through the archway to the courtyard and your neat, tiled room. Swallows nest in the age-old beams and eaves of the house and verandas, while quiet men rake the gravel and tend the beautiful formal gardens and lawns.

In the heat of summer, nothing could be more calming than to take your iced *fino* to the colonnaded terrace overlooking the trees and flowers and to sit in a padded wicker armchair for an hour or so before dinner. The dining-room is quite informal and – please note – is open only at the height of the season; but lazy breakfasts can be enjoyed into the late morning, making the most of the excellent fresh coffee and newly baked rolls, croissants and sweet cakes.

Nearby Cambados – *pazos* and restaurants (10 km); beaches at San Vicente do Mar (5 km).

36990, Villalonga, Pontevedra
Tel (986) 743000
Location a short way up hill overlooking town; with gardens and car parking
Meals breakfast, lunch, dinner
Prices rooms 4,750-7,250pts; breakfast 450pts; meals 2,450pts
Rooms 22 double, all with bath; all rooms have central heating, phone
Facilities dining-room, sitting-room, bar, terrace; tennis court, swimming-pool
Credit cards MC, V
Children tolerated
Disabled some ground-floor rooms
Pets not accepted
Closed Oct to May
Proprietor Luis Ansorena Garret

Pontevedra

Historic Parador, Pontevedra

PN Casa del Barón

The approach to Pontevedra is not promising: the roads are extremely busy and smoke belches from a cement works. But, as so often in Spain, as soon as you turn into the old town, you are suddenly immersed in another world, with cobbled streets and shutters, balconies and stone façades which tell of a different way of life.

The Parador is at the heart of Pontevedra's old town, and is one of the most captivating of the chain, occupying a beautiful old *pazo* which has been the home of many grandees. It is not imposing, but rather elegant, with plenty of antiques which are meant to be used rather than just admired, giving you the feeling that this is a place where you should know how to behave – the suites in the sitting-rooms are covered in apricot-coloured suede, for example.

The dining-room is hung with tapestries and chandeliers, gilt mirrors and paintings, and overlooks the terraced garden with its fountain and rosebeds. As with many of the Paradores there are regional dishes on the menu and at the Casa del Barón this may include *lamprea* (lamprey), which can be very rich and is something of an acquired taste.

Nearby Museo Provincial; Mirador de Coto Redondo (15 km).

Calle Maceda, 36002, Pontevedra
Tel (986) 855800
Location on cobbled street in heart of old town; with garden and car parking in courtyard
Meals breakfast, lunch, dinner
Prices rooms 8,000-10,000pts; breakfast 1,100pts; dinner 3,200pts
Rooms 44 double, 3 single, all with bath; all rooms have central heating, phone, TV, minibar
Facilities dining-room, 2 sitting-rooms, bar, conference room
Credit cards AE, DC, MC, V
Children welcome
Disabled lift/elevator
Pets not accepted
Closed never
Manager José Basso Puga

Orense

Modern hilltop Parador, Verín

PN Monterrey

The 'Monterrey' Parador is named after the dramatic castle which occupies a neighbouring hilltop, and which you can see for many miles before you reach the town of Verín. Parts of the castle church date back to the 13th century and there are towers from the 16th and 17th centuries. The whole complex was abandoned around a hundred years ago but the fortifications are now undergoing restoration.

In contrast, the Parador is a relatively recent construction, though it has been built in local stone with concessions to regional architectural style and it sits happily on its own hilltop surrounded by trees and lawns. As Paradores go it is undistinguished and is scarcely a place to spend the whole of your holidays, but the swimming-pool, the breezy setting and the nearby sights make it worthy of a short stopover.

The old town of Verín itself is quiet and picturesque, and the valley of the Támega river which runs off north from here is lined with vineyards. Wines from nearby which appear on the Parador list and which are worth trying include the lovely fruity whites from Ribeiro.

Nearby Mineral water spas at Sousas, Cabreiroa and Villaza, and bottling factory at Fontenova (5 km).

32600, Verín, Orense
Tel (988) 410075
Location on hill above town; with garden and car parking
Meals breakfast, lunch, dinner
Prices rooms 7,500-9,500pts; breakfast 1,000pts; meals 3,000pts
Rooms rooms 22 double, one single, all with bath; all rooms have central heating, phone, TV, minibar
Facilities dining-room, sitting-room, bar, terrace; swimming-pool
Credit cards AE, DC, MC, V
Children accepted
Disabled some ground-floor bedrooms
Pets not accepted
Closed never
Manager Jesus Santa Maria

41

León

Town hotel, Valencia de Don Juan

Hostal El Palacio

For the last 23 summers the Eguens have devotedly run this welcoming but little-known hotel which specializes in excellent, wholesome home cooking and cider.

As an Asturian, José Manuel Eguen knows practically everything there is to know about the bottle. In the old stables at the back he has built himself a *sidrería* – a bar – out of black wood seasoned with the smell of cider. It is also a fascinating folk museum; on the walls you will find a prehistoric one-way telephone and an ancient precursor of the Thermos flask.

The house is probably the oldest in the village, certainly the only one bearing a coat of arms. King Felipe III is supposed to have stopped off here once upon a time and seduced the mistress of the house; there is a framed document in the hall to prove it. The patio – shaded by Virginia creeper and vines – has an old cart in one corner, painted bright red and green, and a five-foot-long blacksmith's bellows in another. A cool and attractive alternative to the dining-room and sitting-room, it is looked down upon by a wide iron-railinged balcony on the first floor: both are pleasant places to sit. The rooms are light, cheerful and spotlessly clean; prepared, perhaps, more with love than taste.

Nearby Castle; León (30 km); San Miguel de Escalada (45 km).

Calle Palacio 3, 24200,
Valencia de Don Juan, León
Tel (987) 750474
Location in centre of town;
car parking in street
Meals breakfast, lunch, dinner
Prices rooms 2,400-4,400pts
(half-price for children);
breakfast 350pts, dinner
1,000pts
Rooms 8 double, 2 single, all
with bath; all rooms have
phone

Facilities dining-room,
sitting-room, bar, patio
Credit cards AE, DC, MC, V
Children welcome
Disabled access difficult
Pets not accepted
Closed winter months
Proprietor José Manuel Eguen

León

Town hotel, Valencia de Don Juan

Hotel Villegas II

Villegas II looks and sometimes feels more like a private house in its own grounds than a hotel. You might even drive past it, as we did, without noticing the blue hotel plaque by the door. From its external appearance you would expect the hotel to be pleasant and home-like inside, and it does not disappoint. The entrance hall is dominated by blue tiles and light wrought iron, and lit by a stained glass skylight. Neo-Arabic arches lead to the bar, dining-room and a small lounge.

All of the bedrooms give on to the garden. They have been decorated with some flair; the bedspreads and curtains are white-and-blue flowered, much of the furniture is of light wood and the doors and door-frames are of stripped pine.

Outside, there is a fringe of garden all round the building, which takes in a swimming-pool and an outdoor dining-terrace.

This hotel is everything that the Palacio (see separate entry) over the road is not. Here you can choose between two facing hotels – both charming in different ways. (Villegas I, by the way, is something else again: a modern multi-storey block down the road.)

Nearby Castle (short walk); León (30 km); San Miguel de Escalada (45 km); Astorga (55 km).

Calle Palacio 17, 24200, Valencia de Don Juan, León
Tel (987) 750161
Location in centre of town; with garden and car parking
Meals breakfast, lunch, dinner
Prices rooms 6,000-8,000pts; breakfast 300pts, dinner 1,500pts
Rooms 5 double, one family room, all with bath; all rooms have central heating, phone, TV

Facilities dining-room, sitting-room, bar, terrace; swimming-pool
Credit cards AE, DC, MC, V
Children welcome; garden play area
Disabled access difficult
Pets not accepted
Closed Dec to Feb
Proprietor Felisa Garcia Astorga

43

León

Town hotel, Astorga

Hotel Gaudí

The Hotel Gaudí is right in the middle of Astorga, on the main square which has seen the meeting of Roman roads, the passing of pilgrims on their way to Santiago, and the building of the extraordinary Episcopal Palace. The Hotel takes its name from the Barcelona architect, Antonio Gaudí, who built this wildly decorated pastiche of a Gothic palace in 1889. It now houses a museum about the pilgrim ways to Santiago de Compostela.

This stylish, recently built hotel offers comforts far removed from the sort of conditions those earlier travellers would have encountered. The elegant restaurant, with its marble floor, chandeliers and panelled walls, overlooks the square – as does the bar area, which serves excellent *tapas*. Many of the bedrooms have balconies, their shutters opening on to views of the huge and complicated cathedral, with its flying buttresses and carvings, the Gaudí palace and the surrounding terracotta roofs above narrow, cobbled lanes. They are individually furnished and most are carpeted, which makes a pleasantly soft change after the bare boards and marble floors of so many Spanish hotels.

The quiet square is mostly used as a car park and is bordered by trees, shrubs and flowers, cafés and shops.

Nearby León (40 km).

Plaza Eduardo de Castro 6,
24700, Astorga, León
Tel (987) 615654
Location in main square near cathedral and Gaudí palace; with car parking in square
Meals breakfast, lunch, dinner
Prices rooms 7,000-7,500pts; breakfast 450pts; meals 1,100pts
Rooms 35 double, all with bath; all rooms have central heating, phone, TV, radio

Facilities dining-room, sitting-room, bar
Credit cards AE, DC, MC, V
Children accepted
Disabled access difficult
Pets not accepted
Closed never
Manager José Ramón Jarrin Alonso

León

Modern Parador, Villafranca del Bierzo

PN de Villafranca del Bierzo

In days gone by, Villafranca del Bierzo was a stopping place for pilgrims on their way to Santiago de Compostela; today, trucks and tourists roar through on the NVI highway on their way from La Coruña and Lugo to Madrid.

The Parador is a modern, low, white building with colourful flowerbeds and a small terrace – not a particularly notable example of the breed, and certainly not a destination in itself, but a pleasant enough spot for an overnight stop between the holiday highlights of the Picos de Europa mountains to the east and the Galician coast to the west. It is on the outskirts of the town, overlooking the valley, with its light industry, saw mills, road and rail links. But beyond these 20thC intrusions the hills rise from the valley floor to the foothills of the wild Cordillera Cantabrica, north of the town, and to the mountains of León to the south.

As usual the restaurant here tries to present some local delicacies: besides the fish of the region – trout and salmon in particular – the terraced hillsides of the Sil river valley produce clean dry white Palomino wines and some pleasant light reds.

Nearby 10thC monastery of San Genadio in the Valley of Silence, Peñalba de Santiago (45 km).

Avenue de Calvo Sotelo, 24500, Villafranca del Bierzo, León
Tel (987) 540175
Location off main road in small agricultural town; with garage and car parking
Meals breakfast, lunch, dinner
Prices rooms 7,000-8,500pts; breakfast 1,000pts; meals 3,000pts
Rooms 29 double, 10 single, one suite, all with bath; all rooms have central heating, phone, TV
Facilities dining-room, sitting-room, bar
Credit cards AE, DC, MC, V
Children welcome
Disabled some ground-floor rooms
Pets not accepted
Closed never
Manager Juan Comino García

Cantabria

Mountain hotel, Cosgaya

Hotel del Oso

You will already have come through some exceptional scenery to reach Cosgaya, climbing steadily all the way from the coast, and once you arrive you are surrounded by peaks, many snow-covered until early summer.

A small bridge over a clear mountain stream takes you into the forecourt of this stone-built hotel, with its wooden balconies, arched veranda and overflowing flowerpots. The public rooms are cool and dark in the summer heat, but cosy and welcoming in the winter, with log fires in the sitting-room. Although the hotel has only recently been built, it is traditional in style with plenty of workmanship to admire, in wood, terracotta tiling and bare stonework. The restaurant, too, makes use of regional specialities – fresh river trout, interesting local cheeses and regional wines.

There is always the chance of getting snowed in when staying in this area, so bring plenty of books – it has been known to happen in June, though at that time of year you are more likely to be lazing around their pool, playing tennis or off hiking in the hills. They are used to British visitors here, and good English is spoken at the desk.

Nearby Cable-car at Fuente De (10 km) to 1800 m.

39539, Cosgaya, Cantabria
Tel (942) 730418
Location by stream in mountains; with garden and car parking
Meals breakfast, lunch, dinner
Prices rooms 4,600-7,200pts; breakfast 475pts, dinner 1,600-2,200pts
Rooms 32 double, 4 single, all with bath; all rooms have central heating, phone
Facilities dining-room, 3 sitting-rooms, bar; swimming-pool, tennis court
Credit cards DC, MC, V
Children welcome
Disabled access difficult
Pets not accepted
Closed 15 Jan to 15 Feb
Proprietor Severo Rivas Marcos

Cantabria

Historic Parador, Santillana del Mar

PN Gil Blas

On a fleeting visit, Santillana can seem like an overpopulated film set, but if you stay overnight you will have opportunity and time to take in the essence of the place. The Parador Gil Blas – one of the most captivating of the Paradores – is without doubt the place to stay if you have the choice.

Gil Blas was the fictional hero of a story by the French writer Lesage, a fact seemingly unconnected with the house itself, which was the country home of the Barreda Bracho family, built in the 15th and 16th centuries. The worn stone, the lovely terracotta roof tiles, the delightful courtyard garden and the cobbled entrance hall are all in harmony with the medieval atmosphere of the village.

There are two parts to this Parador – the original fine old manor house right in the centre of Santillana del Mar, and the new annexe across the square. It would not be a complete disaster if you ended up with a new room, but the character of Gil Blas is something special and the rooms are exceptional; many have long windows and balconies but the ones overlooking the garden are probably the most pleasant.

Nearby Villas House, Calle de Santo Domingo; Velarde Tower, Plaza de Las Arenas; Altamira cave exhibition (5 km).

Plaza Ramón Pelayo 11, 39330, Santillana del Mar, Cantabria
Tel (942) 818000
Location on main square in heart of village; with garden and garage
Meals breakfast, lunch, dinner
Prices rooms 9,500-14,000pts; breakfast 1,100pts; meals 3,200pts
Rooms 47 double, 5 single, 4 suites; all rooms have central heating, phone, TV, minibar
Facilities dining-room, sitting-room, breakfast room, bar, conference room
Credit cards AE, DC, MC, V
Children accepted
Disabled no special facilities
Pets not accepted
Closed never
Manager Juan María Garralda Ibarren

Cantabria

Village hotel, Santillana del Mar

Hotel Altamira

If you want to be right in the heart of the old village of Santillana del Mar, in an old house which has retained much of its character whilst offering full facilities, but you have had enough of Paradores, then the Hotel Altamira will probably suit you.

The hotel has recently been extended to take in the house next door, and has a large courtyard garden at the back which doubles as a terrace for outside dining or drinking when the weather is right. The place has a comfortable air of antiquity, with old chests, chairs, paintings and mirrors dotted around, but is not at all like a museum.

The restaurant is in country style, with red and white cloths and tiled floors, the breakfast room quiet, dark and green, under lovely stone arches. The wooden stairs – pleasantly creaky, with nicely old-fashioned flowered carpet – lead from the stone-flagged entrance hall up to the sitting-rooms and bedrooms which are found off at interesting angles and on different levels. The bedrooms themselves are furnished in keeping with the atmosphere of the house, with its polished wood floors, beams and, in places, bare stone walls.

Nearby Villas House, Calle de Santo Domingo; Velarde Tower, Plaza de Las Arenas; Altamira cave exhibition (5 km).

Cantón 1, 39330, Santillana del Mar, Cantabria
Tel (942) 818025
Location in old village, on road to church; no private car parking
Meals breakfast, lunch, dinner
Prices rooms 3,500-9,500pts; breakfast 425pts; meals 1,475pts
Rooms 18 double, 5 single, 2 suites, 6 family rooms, all with bath; all rooms have central heating, phone, TV, hairdrier
Facilities dining-room, sitting-room, bar, terrace, conference room
Credit cards AE, DC, MC, V
Children accepted
Disabled access difficult
Pets small dogs accepted
Closed never
Manager David Oceja Bujan

Cantabria

Village hotel, Santillana del Mar

Los Infantes

The Hotel Los Infantes, set slightly back from the main road, just outside the village of Santillana del Mar, has been built around a lovely old 18thC stone country house. Entering the hall from the terrace through a decorated stone archway you can sense the grandeur of the old ways of life. There are huge carved chests on stone floors, and wrought iron chandeliers hanging from high ceilings with massive wooden beams. The bar is in this lobby area, and you can sink into a deep leather armchair and soak up the atmosphere here or take your drink out into the sheltered garden. The upstairs sitting-room also has leather armchairs, as well as more formal reproduction furniture. At the height of the season there is a disco-bar in the cellars.

The restaurant is modern and unfussy, in café style. Many of the bedrooms are rather undistinguished, with uniform bright yellow bedspreads and small bathrooms, but if you go overboard and have a suite it is a different story: individually furnished rooms with antique bed-heads, paintings on the walls, hand-woven bedspreads, comfortable chairs, carpets, balconies and large, immaculate bathrooms.

Nearby sights of Santillana del Mar; Altamira cave exhibition (5 km).

Avenida Le Dorat 1, 39330, Santillana del Mar, Cantabria
Tel (942) 818100
Location on main road past village; parking for 20 cars
Meals breakfast, lunch, dinner
Prices rooms 3,000-11,000pts; breakfast 480pts; meals 1,800pts
Rooms 27 double, 3 single, all with bath; all rooms have central heating, phone, TV
Facilities dining-room, sitting-room, bar/disco
Credit cards AE, DC, MC, V
Children accepted
Disabled ground-floor rooms
Pets by arrangement only
Closed never
Proprietor Gervasio Mesones Canales

Cantabria

Village hotel, Santillana del Mar

Hotel Santillana

The Hotel Santillana is right on the corner of the main road going past Santillana and the turning for the caves at Altamira, so you take your life in your hands every time you step out of the front door (there is no pavement) and rooms on the road may be noisy, particularly at the height of the season; but, in compensation, the rooms are (by a narrow margin) the cheapest of our Santillana hotels.

The neat, stone-built hotel does have some character, and inside there are plenty of old portraits and antiques, some of which are showing signs of wear – perhaps part of the reason for the hotel's two-star grading. There is a large and busy bar with a cafeteria serving snacks all day, as well as a restaurant for evening meals, both of which are in modern bistro style and cater for non-residents as well as guests. The bedrooms are simply furnished but have more character than in many hotels of this type, with antique bedsteads, and original paintings on the walls; several have new bathrooms.

When we visited there was some building going on at the back of the hotel which did not encourage long morning lie-ins.

Nearby sights of Santillana del Mar; Altamira cave exhibition (5 km).

El Cruce, 39330, Santillana del Mar, Cantabria
Tel (942) 818011
Location on crossroads at entrance to old village
Meals breakfast, lunch, dinner
Prices rooms 2,700-8,500pts; breakfast 425pts; meals 1,600pts
Rooms 31 double, 7 single, all with bath; all rooms have central heating, phone; 10 rooms have TV

Facilities dining-room, sitting-room, bar
Credit cards AE, DC, MC, V
Children accepted
Disabled no special facilities
Pets accepted
Closed never
Proprietor Gervasio Mesones Canales

Cantabria

Hostal Luzón

On the main square in San Vicente de la Barquera, the Luzón is an imposing old house set in a prettily kept flower-garden. The main hall and the sitting-room are grand, with polished marble floors, chandeliers, gilt mirrors and comfortable chairs. By comparison the bedrooms are disappointing, tending to mustiness and showing definite signs of age, such as chipped bathroom tiles. The lack of a restaurant is not a problem – San Vicente is packed with good places to eat, including a delightful pastry shop right across the square from the hostal.

Nearby Pumalverde church and viewpoint (25 km); Comillas (10 km) with park and buildings by Gaudí.

Av Miramar 1, 39540, San Vicente de la Barquera, Cantabria
Tel (942) 710050
Location on main square in heart of town; with car parking on street
Meals breakfast
Prices rooms 4,000-6,000pts; breakfast 400pts
Rooms 29 double, 7 single, all with bath; all rooms have central heating, phone
Facilities dining-room, sitting-room
Credit cards not accepted
Children welcome
Disabled no special facilities
Pets not accepted
Closed never
Proprietor Maria del Carmen Diez Postigo

Hotel Miramar

The Miramar is a modern and not particularly charming hotel but it is far from being a seaside monstrosity (it has a pitched roof) and it does have a spectacular position above the estuary at San Vicente de la Barquera, an interesting old port capped with ancient fortifications. Its other chief attraction is its restaurant, which shares the views and makes the most of the seafood fresh from the harbour; lobsters are kept alive in a tank in the garden. The rooms are rather simple, but they all have balconies (not all with sea views).

Nearby Sable del Merón beach (5 km); Church of Santa Maria de los Angeles and 8thC castle, San Vicente de la Barquera.

39540, San Vicente de la Barquera, Cantabria
Tel (942) 710075
Location on west bank of river mouth; with car parking
Meals breakfast, lunch, dinner
Prices rooms 3,900-5,200pts; breakfast 550pts; meals 1,760pts
Rooms 13 double, 2 single, all with bath; all rooms have central heating, phone, TV
Facilities dining-room, sitting-room, bar
Credit cards AE, DC, MC, V
Children accepted
Disabled no special facilities
Pets not accepted
Closed never
Proprietor Juan José Noriega Rancaño

Vizcaya/Navarra

Hotels from Vizcaya to Navarra

Visitors from Britain tend to overlook the Basque country just over the French border in their hurry to explore the Picos or the coastline of Galicia to the west. Yet it has a lot to offer. Not least of the attractions is the smart seaside resort of San Sebastián (or Donostia – duplicate names are a constant reminder here of the Basque separatist movement). In a region noted for fine food, this is probably the gastronomic headquarters; sadly, none of the best restaurants have rooms. Two places to stay stand out, neither of them cheap: the big and charmless Monte Igueldo, which enjoys a heart-stopping view (especially at night) from the peak of the same name at one side of the sweeping Bahía de la Concha (Tel (943) 210211); and the lovely old seafront Hotel de Londres y de Inglaterra (Tel (943) 426989), as gracious a seaside hotel as you could wish for.

Close to the French border is the little fortified town of Fuenterrabía (or Hondarribia), with a splendid ancient Parador at its heart. Since the Parador has only 16 rooms, alternatives are often necessary; the Jauregui is a simpler recommendable place (Tel (943) 641400), but we have recently heard good reports of the Pampinot – an up-market little hotel (only 8 rooms) in a beautifully renovated old mansion (Tel (943) 640600). It does not have a restaurant, which creates the ideal excuse for eating at the local Michelin-starred place, Ramón Roteta.

To the south, neither the top-rated wine area of La Rioja nor its up-and-coming neighbour, Navarra, are geared up for visitors in the way that Bordeaux and Burgundy are. But there is some splendid scenery, and Navarra has some notable hotels. These include a Parador occupying part of a fairytale castle at Olite, and another (but quite different) opportunity to combine sight-seeing with hotel-going at the remote Monasterio de Leyre: the lovely crypt is worth the journey, and the monks run a 30-room Hospedería where you can spend the night in simple comfort (Tel (948) 884100).

Thanks largely to Hemingway's novels, Pamplona is world-famous for its July fiesta and associated barbaric bull-running. It has several glossy big hotels, none of them particularly recommendable. Save a few pounds and stay at the equally big (150-room) but simpler and traditionally stylish Maisonnave (Tel (948) 222600) or (for ready access to the Plaza de Toros) the smaller Orhi, without restaurant (Tel (948) 228500).

Our explorations of La Rioja have thrown up hardly any notable hotels, which makes it particularly regrettable that the Parador at Santo Domingo de la Calzada has been closed. Neither of the big wine towns, Logroño and Haro, has anything special to offer.

Hotel prices
As we explain in the Introduction, many hotels did not know their 1992 prices when we were preparing this edition. It is always wise to check room prices when making a booking or taking a room: hotels sometimes change their prices by much more than inflationary amounts. And Italian hotel prices are particularly likely to change this year.

Burgos

Roadside hotel, Burgos

Hotel Landa Palace

Forget real palaces for a moment; this is the eccentric dream of one Señora Landa. Some consider it luxurious, charmingly over-the-top or supremely pretentious; we see it as great fun. A sense of excess is aroused by the prodigious collection of old horse carts outside; but inside you are positively whisked away from reality into a Gothic fantasy. The tower you step into, transported to this convenient roadside location from a neighbouring village, is the only genuinely old part of the hotel. All the rest – including the Gothic vaults over the larger dining-room and the swimming-pool, and the carved spiral staircases – is a mere 25 years old.

The bedrooms are no less excessive. The grand suite has doors of polished walnut and a brass bedstead surmounted by a crown. Its sitting room – containing a massive antique desk and five-seater settee – could house a numerous family. But don't look out of the romantic, *ajimez* window or the spell will be broken by the sight of the main Burgos-Madrid road.

There are antiques and greenery everywhere, and surprises at every turn. The corridor outside the dining-rooms ticks to the rhythm of umpteen wall clocks.

Nearby Burgos; Miraflores Carthusian Monastery (5 km).

Carretera Madrid, 09000, Burgos
Tel (947) 206343
Location on main road to Madrid; with garden and car parking
Meals breakfast, lunch, dinner
Prices rooms 12,000-35,000pts; breakfast 1,200pts, dinner 6,500pts
Rooms 32 double, 3, single, 7 suites, all with bath; all rooms have central heating, air-conditioning, phone, TV; most rooms have hairdrier
Facilities dining-room, 2 sitting-rooms, bar
Credit cards AE, DC, MC, V
Children welcome; baby-sitting available
Disabled access easy; lift/elevator
Pets not accepted
Closed never
Manager Victoria Landa

Burgos

City hotel, Burgos

Mesón del Cid

Opposite the Cathedral and on its own little square, this hotel looks like a pleasingly proportioned, much overgrown cottage. Its owner is a book-collector – most appropriate, as Burgos is a city associated with early printing – and almost the first thing that you will see inside is a reproduction of an illuminated manuscript on display in the hall. Not, as it turns out, the famous El Cid poem, which is the theme of the rest of the hotel.

Although less than ten years old, the building has been decorated with great style and sensitivity. The floors and bedrooms are named after kings, queens and other characters from El Cid. Particularly striking are the bathrooms, with out-of-the-ordinary matt porcelain basins and chunky brass taps. The bedroom furniture is antique or reproduction, with iron and brass bedsteads and some fine details such as a black-and-brass phone in one room.

Best of the public rooms is the basement bar with black chairs and marble-topped tables. The next-door disco doubles inadequately as a sitting-room. The dining-room upstairs is rectangular and low-ceilinged; there is also a separate public restaurant, connected to the hotel by a passageway, with a choice of rooms.
Nearby Cathedral; Miraflores Carthusian Monastery (4 km).

Plaza Santa Maria 8, 09000, Burgos
Tel (947) 208715
Location in front of cathedral in city centre; with private garage
Meals breakfast, lunch, dinner
Prices rooms 6,900-17,500pts; breakfast 850pts, dinner 3000pts
Rooms 21 double, 5 single, 3 suites, all with bath; all rooms have central heating, phone,
TV, radio
Facilities dining-room, sitting-room/disco, bar
Credit cards AE, DC, MC, V
Children welcome; baby-sitting available
Disabled access easy; lift/elevator
Pets accepted
Closed never
Proprietor José Lopez Alzaga

Burgos

Hotel Cordón

Behind its sober façade, the Cordón is a modern place decorated with unusual discretion. Its walls are in soothing tones of cream and brown, the floors and furniture are black-and-white checks, and the upholstery is tastefully striped in grey. Most of the rooms have parquet floors and modern light-wood furnishings; some have balconies or bay windows looking over the street. They are comfortable without being cosy, although the singles are somewhat cramped. On the top floor are attic rooms with sloping roofs. For no-nonsense city-centre accommodation, you could scarcely do better.

Nearby Cathedral; Miraflores Carthusian monastery (4 km).

La Puebla 6, 09004, Burgos
Tel (947) 265000
Location near Plaza de Calvo Sotelo, in middle of city; with public parking nearby
Meals breakfast
Prices rooms 5,200-8,800pts; breakfast 550pts
Rooms 32 double with bath; 3 single with shower; all rooms have central heating, phone, TV, radio; some rooms have hairdrier, minibar
Facilities sitting-room, cafeteria
Credit cards AE, DC, MC, V
Children welcome
Disabled access easy; lift available
Pets accepted in bedrooms only
Closed never
Manager Carlos Fuentes

Paradores in North Central Spain

Those who arrive in Spain on the Santander ferry are in reach of three Paradores. The PN Gil Blas at Santillana del Mar (see page 47) is one of the best of the chain. The others are modern, but enjoy enviable positions in the mountains of the Picos de Europa. The otherwise dreary PN Río Deva at Fuente Dé is spectacularly set high up in a natural amphitheatre, close to a cable-car giving access to wonderful views and walks (Tel (942) 730001). PN Fuentes Carrionas is further south at Cervera de Pisuerga in the less spectacular foothills of the Picos, but is a rather more stylish hotel (Tel (988) 870075).

East and south-east of Santander are some wonderfully historic Paradores. The oldest, PN El Emperador at Fuenterrabía, is built in the remains of a 10thC fortress whose crumbling ten-foot thick walls are in constant need of restoration. It is high on our agenda for inspection for a future edition (Tel (943) 642140). The PN de Argómaniz, east of Vitoria, has 54 rooms in wings built on to a mellow 300-year-old mansion; service is reported to be 'good and friendly' (Tel (945) 282200). South of Pamplona is the PN Príncipe de Viana at Olite (medieval capital of Navarra), a fairy-tale castle of turrets and towers, with some splendid rooms within (Tel (948) 740000). The PN Marco Fabio Quintiliano at nearby Calahorra in La Rioja is a modern building of five floors with 63 rooms (Tel (941) 130358).

Burgos

Village hotel, Covarrubias

Hotel Arlanza

The Arlanza takes up one side of an attractive cobbled square (closed to traffic) in a clean, prettily restored village full of half-timbered houses, shady porticoes and balconies decked with flower pots.

It is not one of those hotels brimming over with space and facilities, and is all the more refreshing for this. But, with black beams overhead and a handsome, wide, tiled staircase, it has some character. The sitting room, unfortunately, is combined with the bar, and there is nowhere else pleasant to sit. But you will eat well in the dining-room, which is dimly lit by one small window. The Castilian soup is served so hot that it has to be eaten with a wooden spoon. Wild boar – plentiful in these parts, and a nocturnal traffic hazard until the start of the hunting season – is served in rich savoury slices.

The bedrooms, leading off dark corridors paved with squeaky red tiles, are very simply furnished. There is an occasional clash of striped and stippled marbles and the bathrooms are in need of improvement. But you get no more or less than you need for a comfortable night.

Nearby Santo Domingo de Silos and Yecla Gorge (20 km), Quintanilla de las Viñas (25 km).

Plaza del Doña Urraca, 09346, Covarrubias, Burgos
Tel (947) 403025
Location on main square; no car parking in square
Meals breakfast, lunch, dinner
Prices rooms 4,400-7,600pts; breakfast 550pts, dinner 1,700pts
Rooms 34 double, 32 with bath, 2 with shower; 4 single, 2 suites, all with bath; all rooms have central heating, phone

Facilities 2 dining-rooms, sitting-room, bar
Credit cards AE, DC, MC, V
Children welcome
Disabled access easy; lift/elevator
Pets accepted
Closed Dec to Mar
Proprietor Juan José Ortiz

Burgos

Village hotel, Santo Domingo de Silos

Hotel Tres Coronas de Silos

A charming, peaceful establishment, so unpretentious that it doubles as the village newsagents, this is the place to come if you want to be undisturbed. You can hear the birds singing – though in high season you must wait until the coach parties go home.

The hotel is the dominant house on the village square, with a semi-circular arched doorway and a proud coat of arms over its central balcony (which belongs to room number 9, by the way). Inside, there is an overwhelming effect of renovated stone and ancient, seasoned wood (all of it skilful reproduction). Each of the rooms has at least one bare stone wall, an ample ration of solid furniture and a large, tinted mirror. Those at the front of the building look out on to the square through leaded lights fringed with stained glass.

The bar is small, frequently dominated by the TV and insufficiently lit to write in, and the only sitting-area is on the second floor landing. The dining-room includes its own wood-fired roasting oven. (But for half the price of a menu here you can get a good, although more casual, meal in the Hostal Santo Domingo de Silos, a minute's walk away, prepared and served by a delightfully jolly landlady.)

Nearby Monastery and cloister; Yecla Gorge (5 km).

Plaza Mayor 6, 09610, Santo Domingo de Silos, Burgos
Tel (947) 380727
Location near monastery, in main square; car parking on square
Meals breakfast, lunch, dinner
Prices rooms 4,000-7,400pts; breakfast 625pts; dinner 2,500-3,000pts
Rooms 14 double, 2 single, all with bath; all rooms have central heating, phone

Facilities dining-room, bar
Credit cards AE, DC, MC, V
Children welcome
Disabled access impossible
Pets accepted
Closed never
Proprietor Emeterio Martin Garcia

Zaragoza

Former monastery, Nuévalos

Monasterio de Piedra

It is not often that you will find alabaster window panes in a hotel, but glass was not available to the seven Cistercian monks and their abbot who, in the 12th century, founded what is today one of Spain's most intriguing hotels.

The echoing, cavernous corridors – hung with signs imploring silence, and chilly in winter – might as well be time tunnels leading you back to the first millenium AD. If you know where to look, you can still see traces of the castle on top of which the monks built – machicolations and parts of the moat – breaking through centuries of masonry. Beside the cloisters there is a dank Romanesque passageway that may date from as early as the 7th century. The enormous staircase, with vaulting and fading frescoes above will leave you with a stiff neck.

The rooms are varied and unpretentious, their bathrooms nearing the end of their useful lives. Many of the rooms look out on to the beautiful park, full of rocks and waterfalls (visible from the hotel when the leaves fall in autumn), that attracts vast numbers of visitors annually. The best of them is Room 206, on its own entresol up a private staircase.

The hotel is busy with adult education courses in summer.
Nearby Maluenda (40 km); scenic road to Turmiel (45 km).

50210, Nuévalos, Zaragoza
Tel (976) 849011
Location at entrance to park of same name, a few kilometres outside Nuévalos; with garden and car park
Meals breakfast, lunch, dinner
Prices rooms 4,000-11,000pts; breakfast 425pts, dinner 1,900pts
Rooms 44 double, 8 single, 9 family rooms, all with bath; all rooms have central heating,

phone
Facilities sitting-room, bar, TV rooms, games room, terrace
Credit cards AE, DC, MC, V
Disabled access difficult
Pets accepted
Children welcome
Closed never
Manager José Francisco Esponera

Huesca/Lérida

Hotels in Huesca and Lérida

The provinces of Huesca and Lérida are not on the track beaten by most foreign tourists. This is not to say that they have nothing to offer the visitor, but the major attractions are the outdoor activities and scenery of the Pyrenees, the mountains forming the border with France, and rightly or wrongly these are not the usual target of non-Spanish holiday-makers. Not surprisingly, the best hotels are concentrated here, too; access is not easy – even by Alpine standards, the Pyrenean roads can be tortuous and slow – and our inspection tours for this first edition had to miss out several places discussed here which may well merit full entries in future.

The feature box on Paradores in North-east Spain (on page 65) includes several mountain hotels, including the PN del Monte Perdido, just to the east of the spectacular Monte Perdido massif, which forms part of a very impressive National Park. On the other side of the Park there is simple but satisfactory accommodation to be found in and around Torla; the 70-room Ordesa is beautifully situated (Tel (974) 486125). The Paradores at Viella and Arties are mainly ski-oriented; an interesting alternative to the latter for gastronomes (but closed in early summer and early winter) is the Michelin-starred 30-room Valartiés (Tel (973) 640900).

Further east, just to the south of the famously duty-free principality of Andorra (very popular with British skiers), is the historic little city of Seo d'Urgel. In addition to the Parador described elsewhere, it has a pleasant and very comfortable modern hotel in single-storey rustic style, the 40-room El Castell; apart from its mountain situation and corresponding views, the chief attractions are a swimming-pool surrounded by roses and a Michelin-starred restaurant (Tel (973) 350704). A little way further east still, at Martinet on the road to Puigcerda, is another thoroughly comfortable hotel with a highly regarded restaurant, the 35-room Boix (Tel (973) 515050).

The city of Lérida does not attract many visitors and is not notably well prepared to receive them, but Huesca is a pleasant place with some interesting sights. Best-in-town (it does not face much opposition) is the smooth 130-room Pedro I de Aragón, just outside the centre (Tel (974) 220300).

Reporting to the guide

The *Charming Small Hotel Guides* are greatly strengthened by reports from readers. Please write and tell us about your experiences of small hotels, guest-houses and inns, whether good or bad, whether listed in this edition or not. As well as hotels in Spain, we are interested in hotels in Britain and Ireland, Italy, France, Portugal, Austria, Switzerland, Germany and other European countries, and those in the eastern United States. Particularly helpful reporters earn a free copy of the next edition of the guide concerned. And we are always on the lookout for new recruits to our team of inspectors; some undertake trips especially for inspection purposes; while others combine hotel inspections (at our expense, of course) with their own travels.

Tarragona

Country hotel, Espluga de Francoli

Hostal del Senglar

Built in 1965, this three-storey whitewashed and terracotta-roofed hostal is now almost completely obscured by the evergreen trees of its own garden, together with those of the neighbouring civic park. It is a white-walled and wooden-beamed labyrinth inside. The many-chambered dining-hall, with its wooden balconies, nooks, crannies and murals of country scenes, is highly festive when full, and pleasantly intimate when not. The five-course *Menu de Calcotada* is an appropriately medieval feast - a traditional celebration of the vine and onion crops specific to the area (*calcots* is Catalan for shallots). There is yet more timber and pottery in the salon, together with well-upholstered reproduction furniture from which the garden can comfortably be viewed. On Saturday evenings in August there is a splendid barbecue under the trees.

The bright bedrooms have stout wood and leather chairs, and decent-sized tables in addition to good, solid beds. Generous rugs add warmth to the red-tiled floors, and plants, pots and original oil-paintings are dotted around. Señor Lorca Calvo, the suave manager, will smooth over any problems that might arise.

Nearby Poblet Monastery, (2 km); Museum of Rural Life in L'Espluga.

pl Montserrat Canals, 43440, Espluga de Francoli, Tarragona
Tel (977) 870121
Location up hill from main square in civic gardens; with garden and car parking
Meals breakfast, lunch, dinner
Prices rooms 4,850-5,500pts; breakfast 450pts, meals 1,600pts
Rooms 31 double, 10 single, 4 family rooms, all with bath; all rooms have central heating, phone, radio
Facilities dining-room, sitting-room, TV room, disco; swimming-pool, tennis court
Credit cards MC, V
Children welcome; special menus; play area in garden
Disabled access easy; lift/elevator; ground-floor rooms **Pets** accepted in rooms
Closed never
Manager Rafael Lorca Calvo

Tarragona

Mountain hotel, Montblanch

Hotel Coll de Lilla

As the name suggests, this smart, relatively modern roadside lodge, built in traditional Catalan style, occupies a saddle in the mountains that separate Lerida from Tarragona, just above the minuscule hamlet of Lilla. When the mists clear, it commands a tremendous view over Valls to the sea. English-speakers can expect a particularly warm welcome in their own language from Ian Luce. The Coll de Lilla frequently caters for banquets on which occasions the atmosphere is cheerfully hectic; at other times the place is tranquil, almost deserted. The regular through-traffic has of late been somewhat disrupted by closure of the main road, but as this major project nears completion, trade is picking up once again.

Furnishings are modern but sophisticated, with echoes of traditional styles throughout; all the bedrooms are smartly fitted out to a good basic standard. When the wind whistles outside, you can be glad of the central heating and tight-fitting windows. On days such as these the wooden-panelled dining room is the best place to enjoy the view and the more than adequate three-course menu.

Nearby Montblanch (8 km); mountain walks.

Carretera Nacional 240, 43400, Montblanch, Tarragona
Tel (977) 860907
Location on top of pass overlooking valley; with garden and car parking
Meals breakfast, lunch, dinner
Prices rooms 7,000-14,000pts with breakfast; dinner 1,500-3,500pts
Rooms 26 double, all with bath; all rooms have central heating, air-conditioning, phone, TV, minibar, radio
Facilities 2 dining-rooms, 3 conference rooms, gymnasium, sauna; tennis court
Credit cards AE, DC, MC, V
Children welcome; special facilities
Disabled access difficult
Pets not accepted
Closed never
Manager Ian Luce

Tarragona

Hilltop Parador, Tortosa

PN Castillo de la Zuda

On a hilltop, dominating Tortosa and the historic river Ebro below, the Castillo de la Zuda was clearly in a poor state before it was renovated as a Parador. Much of the light stonework appears new. Yet it still retains much of its period feel, with its arched courtyards, cannon, large halls and antiques. The upward climb is steep; once there, all but motorists and the most energetic walkers are effectively trapped. But there are worse places to be imprisoned for a night or two. The bedrooms are typical of Castille: oak-stained furniture and doors, blankets on beds. There are all the usual conveniences, with a touch of luxury in the form of twin basins in the double rooms; terraces afford wonderful views.

Solid Spanish meals with some fish and game specialities are served in the high, timbered-ceiling castle dining-room, brightened with fresh flowers. In classical Parador style, the staff will pay little attention to you as you wander about the bar and salons, swim or even play pool. But if you are lucky enough to catch someone on reception they will invariably smile, and have even been known to get out a map and helpfully point out the way to your next port of call.

Nearby Tortosa – cathedral, chapels and Bishops' Palace.

43500, Tortosa, Tarragona
Tel (977) 444450
Location on hilltop overlooking Tortosa
Meals breakfast, lunch, dinner, snacks
Prices rooms 8,500-11,000pts; breakfast 1,100pts; meals 3,200pts
Rooms 74 double, 8 single, all with bath; all rooms have central heating, air-conditioning, phone, TV;

most have hairdrier, minibar
Facilities dining-room, bar, meeting room; swimming-pool (summer only)
Credit cards AE, DC, MC, V
Children welcome; playground
Disabled access difficult, but lift/elevator to rooms
Pets not accepted
Closed never
Manager Manuel Esteban Hernandez

Barcelona

Hotels in Barcelona

Most of the hotels in the lively and captivating city of Barcelona (host to the 1992 Olympic Games) are in the centre, in two areas – around the Plaça Catalunya and Las Ramblas (the broad, leafy avenue that leads to the sea), and around the cathedral and the medieval quarter (Barrio Gótico).

The Plaça de Catalunya has the more traditional grand hotels, such as the Ritz (Tel (93) 318 5200), an imposing building of 1919 with an abundance of gold-leaf and marble, and recently refurbished palatial rooms making it one of Barcelona's best. The Gran Vía (described on page 64) is another old charmer, as is the Avenida Palace (Tel (93) 301 9600), dignified and extremely popular, with excellent service and welcome. The Regente (Tel (93) 215 2570) has the added bonus of a roof-top swimming-pool. Further out, near the Francescá Macià Plaza, is a very British establishment, the Derby (Tel (93) 322 3215) which is smart and subdued, and, should you be in need, has Guinness on tap.

Of the Barrio Gótico hotels, the Colón (Tel (93) 301 1404) is an old favourite with tourists. It stands opposite the magnificent Gothic cathedral (ask for a front room with a balcony or a sixth-floor room with a terrace) and a stone's throw from many of the city's sights. Rooms have elegant high ceilings and comfortable furniture. The Suizo (described on page 65) is not far from here.

Hotel Gravina

Behind the wrought-iron balconies of its neo-classical façade, the Gravina is modern throughout; the cool, cream marble of the spotless interior dates back to 1988. The main dining-room/salon combines light leather sofas, pink table-cloths, chrome chairs, stone facing on the walls, and dried flowers. There is a pizzeria-cum-bar offering the same meals – a very reasonable three-course menu, plus, in the evenings, an Italian-influenced *carte*. The bedrooms are equally clean and bright, with modern pine, firm beds, brass light fittings, marble bathrooms and all the trimmings (including thick towels).
Nearby Las Ramblas; cathedral and museums.

Calle Gravina 12, 08001, Barcelona
Tel (93) 301 6868
Location in middle of city, near Plaza Universidad, with parking for 10 cars
Meals breakfast, lunch, dinner
Prices rooms 9,900-13,900pts; breakfast 700-1,000pts
Rooms 40 double, 20 single, all with bath and shower; all rooms have central heating, air-conditioning, phone, hairdrier, satellite TV, minibar, radio
Facilities sitting-room, dining-room, pizzeria, cafeteria, meeting room
Credit cards AE, DC, MC, V
Children accepted
Disabled no special facilities
Pets not accepted
Closed restaurant only, Aug
Manager Gerardo Gracia

Barcelona

City hotel, Barcelona

Hotel Gran Vía

In the hell of Barcelona's traffic, the Gran Vía could not be easier to find: entering the city from the airport, on the main street of the same name, you pass it on the right. A large town house, it does not look much from the outside, but once through the double-doored entrance, it is very grand. An impressive staircase sweeps up to the mezzanine, with its palatial dining-room in burgundy and grey and co-ordinating regency chairs. Here, English-speaking guests can have fun explaining to the Spanish-speaking matron who serves the extensive international breakfast how they want their bacon and eggs. Above is another fine room – a salon with stucco ceiling and many antiques – and, true to Spanish form, a huge TV stuck in the middle of the room. Beyond is a gorgeous roof terrace.

The bedrooms, set around the gallery, are variable – from basic to highly elegant-but-worn. The carpets are fraying, the light switches and taps are unreliable, but the air-conditioning is effective, if a bit noisy, and the Gran Vía displays the kind of shabby grandeur that is hard to resist. The staff remember you, and you remember them. The hotel is now under new management; we hope it does not change too much.

Nearby Las Ramblas; cathedral, museums.

Gran Vía 642, 08007, Barcelona
Tel (93) 318 1900
Location set back from Gran Vía, near Plaza Cataluña; with garden and car parking
Meals breakfast only
Prices rooms 10,500-10,500pts; breakfast 525pts
Rooms 37 double, 11 single, all with bath; all rooms have central heating, air-conditioning, phone, minibar
Facilities breakfast-room, sitting/TV room, terrace
Credit cards AE, DC, MC, V
Children accepted
Disabled no special facilities; lift/elevator
Pets not accepted
Closed never
Manager Fernanda Tellez Martinez

Barcelona

City hotel, Barcelona

Hotel Suizo

Just behind the cathedral, the Hotel Suizo could not be better placed. Inside it is really more *Parisien* than Swiss. Marble-topped tables, bentwood chairs and stools line the opulent wooden bar and fill the stylish cafeteria upstairs (where breakfast is served). The large restaurant is invariably busy; the four-course menu offers ample choice and changes daily. Attic bedrooms have the most character, with effective blinds on the skylights, and light parquet floors. Some of the other rooms have lino floors, but all are well furnished in dark oak. The staff can seem somewhat stretched, particularly at check-out time, but are helpful.

Nearby Cathedral, museums, Gothic quarter, Las Ramblas.

Plaza del Angel 12, 08002, Barcelona
Tel (93) 315 4111
Location just behind cathedral; car parking can be arranged
Meals breakfast, lunch, dinner
Prices rooms 9,880-16,250pts; breakfast 675pts; meals 2,750pts
Rooms 44 double, 4 single, all with bath; all rooms have central heating, air-conditioning, phone, TV, minibar, radio
Facilities dining-room, TV room, snack bar
Credit cards AE, DC, MC, V
Children welcome
Disabled access easy; lift/elevator
Pets accepted
Closed never
Manager Miguel Gargallo

Paradores in North-east Spain

The Pyrenees have a handful of remote modern Paradores. The most remote is the PN del Monte Perdido near Bielsa, hidden in a beautiful valley of bubbling mountain streams; the 24 rooms are appropriately rustic and the fireplace is the focal point (Tel (974) 501011). The PN Valle de Arán at Viella and the PN Don Gaspar de Portolá at Arties are separated only by 6 km of bumpy mountain road. Both come into their own in winter, serving the smart ski resort of Baqueira-Beret. The Viella Parador (135 rooms) has a semi-circular glass lounge to allow panoramic views (Tel (973) 640100), and the Arties Parador (40 rooms) is stuffed with hunting trophies and easy chairs (Tel (973) 640801). Just south of Andorra is the PN Seo de Urgel; the modern hotel incorporates an ancient cloister, now filled with trailing plants and functional sofas (Tel (973) 352000).

Further south are two impressive hilltop Paradores, at Cardona and Vich (see pages 66 and 72). And to the west, out of the mountains, the 66-room PN Fernando de Aragón in the captivating hilltop village of Sos del Rey Católico (the famous Fernando's birthplace) – one of the best modern Paradores (Tel (948) 888011).

The modern 87-room PN de la Costa Brava at Aiguablava is chiefly remarkable for its splendid cliff-top setting (Tel (972) 622162). Further south and a little way inland is the PN Castillo de la Zuda at Tortosa (see page 62).

Barcelona

Hilltop Parador, Cardona

PN Duques de Cardona

Perched high on a hill above the Cardener river, this impressive medieval castle, built round an ancient collegiate church with parts dating back to the beginning of the 9th century, commands magnificent views in all directions, including the mountainous slag heaps from the potassium chlorate mine in the valley below.

The church itself is a popular tourist attraction, with guided tours morning and afternoon. But for local Spaniards, and some not so local, the main attraction is the food: an innovative menu and seasonal *carte* of house specialities and rare local dishes – country soups, rich fish stews, and desserts – served in the atmospheric stone-arched halls of the Bodegon restaurant (appropriately named, English-speaking visitors may think). Barcelonians will think nothing of driving the 100 km just to eat here.

There is little concession to medieval asceticism in other respects, though in terms of style, furnishings are faithful to the period of the building. Bedrooms range from extravagant suites with two four-posters to more modest twins, but all are immaculately furnished and clean. The three-chambered sitting-room is all rugs and leather armchairs, and free of TV. Staff put the comfort of their guests first.

Nearby Cardona; Salt Museum; Manresa (32 km).

Castillo, 08261, Cardona, Barcelona
Tel (93) 869 1275
Location on hill top near Cardona, visible for miles; with garden and car parking
Meals breakfast, lunch, dinner
Prices rooms 8,000-10,500pts; breakfast 1,100pts, dinner 3,200pts
Rooms 57 double, all with bath; all rooms have central heating, air-conditioning, phone, TV, minibar
Facilities 2 dining-rooms, sitting-room, cafeteria, patio, 5 conference rooms
Credit cards AE, DC, MC, V
Children welcome
Disabled access difficult
Pets not accepted
Closed never
Manager José Francisco Perez Castillo

Barcelona

Country hotel, Montseny

Hotel Sant Bernat

Hidden away up a tiny track off the winding Tona road, amid the dense low forest of the lush Montseny Sierra, this large, attractive terracotta-roofed villa, built forty years ago and now covered in vines, is a sleepy delight. The grounds are glorious, with a willow tree, pond and fountain to the front, and a stone terrace, and the charming little chapel of Sant Bernat behind. Stand too long admiring the view, or listening to the water trickling down the mountainside, and you are liable to find yourself gradually surrounded by the ancient St Bernard dogs that loll around.

Inside, it is equally serene, though at times the TV in reception is liable to intrude. A series of restful sitting-rooms with fireplaces, leather chairs and rugs lead past the bar to the comfortable dining-room, prettily decorated with floral upholstery, wooden panelled pillars and fresh flowers. The spotless bedrooms are equally attractive, and contain all the extras, from full-length mirrors down to a free comb.

Lunch and dinner involve a three-course fixed menu which changes every day, supplemented by a short but interesting *carte*. There are regular services in the chapel on Sundays and holidays, and special recitals on the feast day of St Bernard in June.
Nearby Montseny (8 km); Montseny Sierra.

08460, Montseny, Barcelona
Tel (93) 847 3011
Location in mountains, up tiny road from Montseny to Tona; with garden and car parking
Meals breakfast, lunch, dinner
Prices rooms 8,230-15,000pts; breakfast 720pts, dinner 2,710pts
Rooms 18 double, 2 family rooms, all with bath; all rooms have central heating, phone,
TV, hairdrier
Facilities dining-room, 2 sitting-rooms, bar
Credit cards MC, V
Children accepted
Disabled no special facilities
Pets not accepted
Closed never
Manager Juan Miguel Perez Vazquez

Barcelona

Seaside hotel, Sitges

La Reserva

Señor Mingels is a genteel man who, like his two-storey villa, is ageing gracefully; but his wife (who is Belgian) is there to keep a sharper eye on the housekeeping. Together with their son, they run this little enclave of 19thC style on the Costa Dorada with calm enthusiasm.

Set in walled gardens at the quiet end of the Sitges promenade overlooking a small sandy bay, the hotel is equipped with a tropical bar, a shaded, lantern-lit, geranium-splashed dining-terrace, a pool and a more recent annexe. The villa itself is a protected historic building – the genuine, slightly decaying article, not for those who want everything spick and span. Inside, there is a small dining-room (for wet days), and the arched living-rooms are pleasantly cluttered with all manner of antique bric-a-brac – the Catalan equivalent of Victoriana.

The bedrooms in the house all share this charming old-fashioned atmosphere; and details such as the old black bakelite phones carry some of the atmosphere through to the annexe. The restaurant at the rear of the garden serves international cuisine, but is open only to guests, (who must take at least half-board). Meals are usually served outside under striped shades.
Nearby beach; central Sitges within walking distance.

passeig Maritim 62, 08870, Sitges, Barcelona
Tel (93) 894 1833
Location on main promenade at south end of beach; with garden and parking for 25 cars
Meals breakfast, lunch, dinner
Prices rooms 4,480-6,910pts; breakfast 561pts, menus 2,105pts
Rooms 24 double, all with bath; all rooms have central heating, phone

Facilities 2 dining-rooms (one on terrace), reception/sitting-room, garden bar; swimming-pool
Credit cards MC, V
Children welcome
Disabled access easy; ground-floor rooms
Pets accepted in rooms
Closed 1 Oct to 30 April
Proprietor Paul Mingels

Barcelona

Seaside hotel, Sitges

Hotel Romàntic

Goncal Sobrer i Barea is passionately in love with his careful restoration of three 19thC town villas, originally built by Catalan rum barons returning from Cuba. He has good cause. This is a real rarity, and, considering it merits, very modestly priced. With its airy halls, blue and white tiles, sculptures, marble bays and ceramics, it could easily be the setting for a novel by García Marquez – or perhaps Graham Greene. In the club-style bar (the bar itself being an original imported from Cuba) you half-expect to spot Our Man From Havana sipping a rum while ensconced in one of the creaking wicker chairs.

Even the old stone washing troughs are preserved (though no longer in use). All the bedrooms are individually furnished with genuine antiques from the period, with original paintings and ceramics. Señor Sobrer is proud that they contain not a single 'mod con' (save, of course, *en suite* bathrooms – only the four single rooms are without), and there are few comfortable sofas; but this is the nineteenth century, after all.

Sadly, only breakfast is served in the palmed, patio-garden these days: a shame, since it would be a most 'romantic' setting for a longer, leisurely meal.

Nearby Old Sitges, museums, main beach.

Sant Isidre 33, 08870, Sitges, Barcelona
Tel (93) 894 0643
Location in side-street in heart of old city; with large garden and car parking
Meals breakfast
Prices 4,500-6,800pts with breakfast
Rooms 47 double, all with bath; 4 single; 4 family rooms, all with bath
Facilities 3 sitting-rooms, bar

Credit cards V
Children welcome; special menus for children under 10
Disabled no special facilities
Pets accepted
Closed 1 Nov to 30 Mar
Proprietor Goncal Sobrer i Barea

Barcelona

Seaside hotel, Sitges

La Santa María

For a restaurant with tables on the seafront in the centre of smart Sitges, the Santa María is refreshingly unpretentious. It is invariably packed, with all kinds of customers enjoying local seafood and wines.

From inside the atmospheric restaurant, glimpses can be caught of the kitchens. Giant wooden fans in the ceiling waft in the smells. Señora Uti – amazingly fluent in English, Spanish, French and German – reserves special treatment for her hotel guests, and is generally to be found behind the bar.

The hotel itself is modern, behind an older five-storey moulded plaster frontage, the chief advantage being that inside it is clean and bright rather than notably well equipped. You will not find air-conditioning or heating in any of the bedrooms, but you will find pleasant wooden furniture, firm beds, good views and plenty of space. Here there is no hint of the restaurant bustle.

In addition, a small TV room with leather armchairs, dotted with antiques, ceramics and magazines, provides a quiet backwater, as does the small sun terrace, where you can be alone with the geraniums.

Nearby Main promenade and beach.

passeig de la Ribera 52, 08870, Sitges, Barcelona
Tel (93) 894 0999
Location on seafront in centre of promenade; public car park nearby
Meals breakfast, lunch, dinner
Prices rooms 4,200-5,500pts; breakfast 600pts, dinner 1,700-2,500pts
Rooms 26 double, 4 single, 5 family rooms, all with bath; all rooms have phone

Facilities dining-room, sitting-room
Credit cards AE, MC, V
Children accepted
Disabled lift/elevator
Pets small dogs accepted
Closed winter
Proprietor Antonìo Arcas Sanchez

Barcelona

Country guest-house, Tavérnoles

El Banús

The ever-smiling Banús family have farmed on this site since 1214, and have a stout family tree proudly displayed in their hall to prove it. The rambling soft-stone farmhouse is modern by comparison – construction started as late as the 15th century. Antonio Banús is still making improvements, with a little help from his son – gently converting an adjoining barn into a dining-room and adding a downstairs room and bathroom for disabled visitors. Meanwhile his wife prepares the solid four-course dinner with similarly traditional skill.

For the time being, the meal is served in the pantry-cum-bar in front of an open fire (highly welcome in winter). The ample breakfasts are also taken here, with a choice of continental bread or *pan con tomate y salchichon*, a local speciality which Antonio insists is nothing like pizza. Rooms, on the second floor, are appropriately basic, with no *en suite* facilities (there are two shared bathrooms) and furnished with a suitably catholic collection of family heirlooms, some delightful. There is no midday meal, but the Banúses are more than happy to provide a picnic for those planning expeditions into the neighbouring foothills. The garden has some deliciously cool corners.

Nearby Vich (8 km); way-marked path to local sights.

08519, Tavérnoles, Barcelona
Tel (93) 888 7012
Location in heart of open countryside near Vich PN; with garden and car parking
Meals breakfast, picnic lunches, dinner
Prices rooms 1,500-3,500pts; breakfast 400pts, dinner 1,200pts; discounts for children
Rooms 6 double, one single, one family room; shared bathrooms; all rooms have central heating
Facilities dining-room, sitting-room, bar; small swimming-pool, table tennis
Credit cards MC, V
Children welcome
Disabled access difficult
Pets well behaved dogs accepted
Closed one week in Sep
Proprietor Antonio Banús Romero

Barcelona

Modern Parador, Vich

PN de Vich

Isolated on a steep mountainside overlooking the expansive Sau reservoir, the Parador de Vich is an imposing grey stone edifice. Completed in 1972 to mimic a Catalan farmhouse, it is quite wrong in scale, but it is nevertheless not without beauty. The conservatory-style entrance gives way to a vast galleried hall with murals, polished wooden pillars and a stained glass ceiling worthy of Chartres.

The sons and daughters from the *masías* dotted throughout the surrounding *sierra* have their wedding receptions here. Walkers and cyclists with sufficient energy come in search of a little luxury and a comfortable bed to rest their limbs. They are rarely disappointed. Rooms are furnished in classical Castilian or Catalan style. Those with larger bathrooms have the unusual luxury of double basins.

The dining-room is another large hall with mock-medieval chandeliers, marble pillars, and more murals. The three-course menu of international, Spanish and Catalan dishes is enhanced by the magnificent view, and as night falls the sounds of the wilderness outside add atmosphere to the occasion. The staff serve with appropriate hushed efficiency.

Nearby Vich (15 km); walks to nearby sights.

Paraje el Bach de Sau, 08500, Vich, Barcelona
Tel (93) 888 7211
Location 14 km E of Vich, clearly signed from Vich; with gardens and parking for 30 cars
Meals breakfast, lunch, dinner
Prices rooms 8,500-12,000pts; breakfast 1,100pts, dinner 3,200pts
Rooms 32 double, 4 single, all with bath; all rooms have central heating, air-conditioning, phone, TV, minibar
Facilities 3 sitting-rooms, bar, dining-room; tennis, swimming-pool
Credit cards AE, DC, MC, V
Children welcome
Disabled access easy; lift available
Pets not accepted
Closed never
Manager Carmelo Martinez

Gerona

Hotels on the Costa Brava

The 'Spanish Riviera' has emerged over the past 30 years as the Costa del Sol's major competitor for Spain's holiday trade. But, unlike the Costa del Sol, it is a naturally rugged coastline of rocky coves, sandy beaches, pine-clad cliffs and little fishing villages. For high season, book well in advance.

Blanes, the 'official' starting point of the Costa Brava, has many inexpensive hotels, pensions and campsites along one of the Costa's longest beaches. One of the best family hotels is the Park Blanes (Tel (972) 330250) secluded in pines, with a swimming-pool, tennis court and children's playground. Further up the coast, Lloret de Mar boasts an even longer beach and a even greater concentration of hotels, restaurants and nightclubs. If you want some solitude, try the 80-room family-owned Santa Marta (Tel (972) 364904), down a winding driveway in an area of private villas and botanical gardens. It is renowned for its sea-food, eaten on the terrace overlooking the beach. Tossa de Mar has several smart little hotels, including three which merit detailed descriptions (pages 73-75). The 74-room S'Agaró hotel (Tel (972) 325200) is a good second best in S'Agaró after the luxurious La Gavina (page 85). North of the Palafrugell area (which has an abundance of places to stay) are many smaller resorts with some reasonable (but not notable) hotels. The Almadraba Park (Tel (972) 256550) is a rather drab 3-storey hotel, but is in a delightfully peaceful spot on the bay of Rosas.

Casa Zügel

A whitewashed building in the centre of Tossa, with pretty blue beams in the eaves and terracotta roof, Casa Zügel encloses a delightful courtyard garden – a controlled chaos of roses, colour and cats. Germans stay here for the simple, but 'proper' rooms, all of which have balconies, most overlooking the garden. Or perhaps for the breakfast of steaming coffee and rolls doled out from the open-to-all-comers kitchen by the Teutonic matron who runs the place. Either way, a few hours spent sitting among the flowers is a holiday in itself. There are also small, simply furnished dining- and sitting-rooms for days when rain stops play.
Nearby Main promenade; town centre; beach.

Avenida de sa Palma 10, 17320, Tossa de Mar, Gerona
Tel (972) 340292
Location 50 metres from the beach; with courtyard garden but no private parking
Meals breakfast
Prices rooms 2,200-4,000pts; breakfast 300pts
Rooms 8 doubles, 4 with bath, 4 with shower; 2 single with bath; 4 family rooms with bath; all rooms have some rooms have central heating
Facilities sitting-room, dining-room
Credit cards none
Children tolerated
Disabled access difficult
Pets not accepted
Closed October to Easter
Proprietor Klara Zügel

Gerona

Seaside hotel, Tossa de Mar

Hotel Diana

After the castle, the Hotel Diana is architecturally one of the most important buildings in Tossa. A family town house built on the central Plaza d'Espana in the 1850s, and backing on to the main promenade, it became a hotel a hundred years later. Today, when it opens for the summer season, it attracts an international clientele of art-nouveau-lovers willing to tolerate the flaking frescos, threadbare carpets and dubious plumbing in order to breakfast in front of the huge, original Gaudi fireplace.

The entire building is a tribute to the period, with a Gaudi roof faced with characteristic broken turquoise tiles, stained glass windows and a sweeping marble staircase. The central salon contains a bronze fountain in naked female form by the Catalan sculptor Mares; light streams in through the glass roof three storeys above. The bedrooms are set in the surrounding gallery. With their high arched ceilings, marble floors and grand wooden shutters, they have plenty to offer in terms of style, although precious little in comfort. Some have reasonable bathrooms.

In 1989, after a period on lease, the Diana was returned to its original owners, a local hotel-owning family who intend to carry out the refurbishment that it so plainly deserves.

Nearby Castle; promenade; central beach.

Plaza d'España 6, 17320, Tossa de Mar, Gerona
Tel (972) 341886
Location entrance on Plaza d'España, rear entrance on beach promenade; no private car parking
Meals breakfast
Prices rooms 4,800-6,800pts; breakfast 500pts
Rooms 19 double, one single, one family room, all with bath
Facilities sitting-room, TV room
Credit cards not accepted
Children welcome
Disabled access easy; lift/elevator
Pets accepted
Closed Oct to Jun
Manager Fernando Osorio Gotarra

Gerona

Seaside hotel, Tossa de Mar

Hostal Roqueta Mar

Eusebio Lazaro met Agnes Greber while working as a chef in Switzerland. In 1981 the two of them took over this modest restaurant with rooms nestled on the steps of the castle above the old town of Tossa de Mar, just off the beaten track. Since then they have gradually built up a solid reputation with their growing list of regular visitors for good housekeeping and no-nonsense food. They offer a choice of two three-course menus, both moderately priced, plus a short *carte* – all good wholesome Spanish stuff.

Rooms are clean, although tiny and basic. The doubles have their own shower, but the singles share a shower between two, and there is a shared lavatory on each floor. The top rooms are the prettiest, with views through the green wooden shutters and exposed beams, the only disadvantage being the extra climb up the quaint but narrow stairs.

Not everyone will find this hostal to their taste, but when enjoying breakfast served on cheerfully set tables on the wisteria-shaded terrace, many will agree that Eusebio and Agnes's establishment retains a seductive Mediterrean simplicity sadly lacking elsewhere on the Costas.

Nearby Old quarter; castle; main beach.

Calle Roqueta 2, 17320, Tossa de Mar, Gerona
Tel (972) 340082
Location on old steps behind castle, close to beach; no private car parking
Meals breakfast, lunch, dinner
Prices rooms 4,000-4,600pts; breakfast 400pts; menus 1,150-1,400pts
Rooms 10 double, all with shower; 4 single, all with basin
Facilities dining-room, bar

Credit cards MC
Children welcome; small beds available
Disabled access difficult
Pets not accepted
Closed Nov to Mar
Proprietor Eusebio Lazaro and Agnes Greber

Gerona

Town hotel, Bagur

Hotel Plaja

The Pujol family have made this appealing *auberge*-like hotel in the heart of old Bagur a modest treat. The two-storey building itself is 80 years old and blends into its surroundings in typical Catalan style. Its pretty terrace with cork trees, roses and tubs of flowers is the main feature of the tiny plaza on to which it looks.

The restaurant inside oozes character, with its sandstone tiles, exposed beams and ceramics displayed in niches set into the walls. There is also a bar in here. Round the corner is a snug little salon with a fireplace, bench seats and more ceremics. Bedrooms are similarly cosy, but good use is made of the limited space, with reproduction pine furniture mixing well with the original pine shutters. There are the attractive, original green-and-white tiles in some of the rooms. Not all have *en suite* facilities though.

The restaurant is popular with residents and non-residents alike. The menu is a four-course affair supplemented by a comprehensive *carte* and local specialities on demand. Zarzuela (Catalonia's answer to bouillabaisse) is a particular favourite. Appetising smells waft from the kitchen at most times of the day. After breakfast a veritable task force of cleaners descend.

Nearby Castle; church; beaches (4 - 5 km).

pl Pella i Forgas, 17255, 17255, Bagur, Gerona
Tel (972) 622197
Location on tiny plaza in heart of old town; with parking for 10 cars
Meals breakfast, lunch, dinner
Prices rooms 4,200-4,800pts; breakfast 450pts, dinner 1,800pts
Rooms 8 double with bath; 8 single, 5 with bath
Facilities TV room

Credit cards MC, V
Children tolerated
Disabled no special facilities
Pets accepted
Closed Christmas
Proprietor Narçis Pujol

Gerona

Town hotel, Bagur

Hotel Begur

Neat signs lead from 2 km out of Bagur to this 25 year-old conversion of a three-storey town house near the centre of the old quarter. Is it a tourist trap, or just a hotel that is unusually well organised? Fortunately, the cheery reception, personal escort to your room, fragrant towels and spotless sheets are quick to convince you that the Hotel Begur is very much the latter.

When we inspected, the immediate surroundings were marred by the construction of an underground car park, but inside, this fine old building retains many original features – central marble stairwell, arched stained glass window, tiled floors – and the character is maintained throughout. Some of the electrics are perhaps a little too antique, and at times the hot water can take a while to make its way through the old pipes, but in general the bedrooms are comfortable and of reasonable size.

The dining-room is smart and cool – netted curtains keep out the sun without obscuring the view. In summer, the substantial Catalan-Spanish three-course menu always starts with a hefty buffet salad. In winter there are soups. If you can find room for a fourth course, a choice can be found on the *carte*. All can be worked off with an evening stroll up to the castle.

Nearby Castle; church; beaches (4-5) km.

Comas y Ros 8, 17255, Bagur, Gerona
Tel (972) 622207
Location on hill by church and below castle, in heart of town; with parking for 6 cars
Meals breakfast, lunch, dinner
Prices rooms 5,980-7,245pts; breakfast 690pts, menus 1,725pts
Rooms 35 double, 29 with bath, 5 with shower; one single with shower; all rooms have central heating, phone, TV
Facilities dining-room, 2 sitting-rooms, bar
Credit cards MC, V
Children welcome
Disabled lift/elevator; 3 ground-floor rooms
Pets accepted
Closed never
Manager Rodolfo Castañer Freìxas

Gerona

Seaside hotel, Aigua Blava

Hotel Aigua Blava

Too big to include in the guide but too distinctive to leave out, the Aigua Blava is a holiday village with a difference – a collection of delightful annexes among shady, pine-covered cliffs and flowered terraces, set round a tiny fishing harbour and beach, the whole the opus of multi-lingual ex-swimming champion, Xiquet Sabater – a man whose life history would defy belief if it were not confirmed in the Spanish *Who's Who?*

The complex provides everything you need, even a boutique complete with genuine French assistance. Each room has individual style, ranging from summerhouse brightness in some annexes to the more formal bedrooms in the main hotel. Even the least inspiring are immaculate, and the sea views are out of this world. Guests who reserve a table in the pleasant terrace restaurant are rewarded with a feast of a four-course meal, with plenty of choice and desserts ranging from the holy to the sinful.

This area has always been Xiquet's home, and he wants his guests to feel the same warmth as if it were theirs, too. If the four generations who come back to this Mediterranean idyll year after year (making early booking essential) are any guide, he succeeds – with abundant help from his cheerful staff.

Nearby Bagur (5 km); beach.

Playa del Fornells, 17255, Aigua Blava, Gerona
Tel (972) 622058
Location in quiet spot near beach; with gardens and car parking
Meals breakfast, lunch, dinner
Prices rooms 5,500-13,400pts; breakfast 1,100pts
Rooms 65 double, all with bath; 6 single, 4 with bath, 2 with shower; 16 suites, all with bath; all rooms have central heating, phone; most rooms have air-conditioning
Facilities 4 dining-rooms, 4 sitting-rooms, 2 bars; swimming-pool, tennis courts, volley ball
Credit cards AE, DC, MC, V
Children welcome; play area and children's swimming-pool
Disabled no special facilities
Pets small dogs accepted
Closed 23 Dec to 21 Mar
Manager Francisco Sabater

Gerona

Country inn, Castelló de Ampurias

Hotel Allioli

The setting for this country inn, in a dusty basin below the main Roses-Figueras road, could be better. But it could also be much worse: the neighbouring blue and white-washed Danone plant is almost picturesque as factories go. And the building itself more than makes up for its surroundings: a two-hundred-year-old Catalan farmhouse of considerable character.

Inside, the Peig Callo family have sympathetically fitted it out with antiques, lamps and benches, spiced up with fresh and dried flowers. Huge, whole dried Jamon Jabugos hams hang over the intimate bar to dry. The bedrooms display pure rural simplicity with linen counterpanes, exposed beams and whitewashed walls. But there are creature comforts too: clean *en suite* bathrooms, plenty of gadgets, and well-placed electric lights.

The beamed four-chambered restaurant is well suited to the vast feasts local Spanish families come to devour on a Sunday. During the week Maria Callo will serve you a quieter, but no less sumptious Catalan meal, or even paella. Breakfast on the patio can be a very pleasant experience, provided the seasonal winds don't blow away your croissant. On such occasions, the bar is a safer alternative.

Nearby Figueras (10 km); Rosas (8 km).

17486, Castelló de Ampurias, Gerona
Tel (972) 250300
Location in grounds set back from main Figueras/Roses road; with car parking
Meals breakfast, lunch, dinner
Prices rooms 2,200-7,000pts; breakfast 500pts, dinner 1,375pts
Rooms 31 double, 8 single, all with bath; all rooms have central heating,
air-conditioning, phone, TV
Facilities 2 dining-rooms, 2 sitting-rooms, bar
Credit cards MC, V
Children accepted
Disabled lift/elevator
Pets accepted in rooms
Closed 17 Dec to 14 Jan
Proprietor José Peig Rions and Maria Callo Fornes

Gerona

Town guest-house, Gerona

Hostal Bellmirall

Anna Pascual and Isdre Vicons run this diminutive guest-house, hidden away just to the right of the cathedral steps, as a family home, which it is. The house is a 14thC historic monument of ancient stone, which Anna and Isdre started converting to take guests 25 years ago; they continue to make minor adjustments to this day. Isdre is supposedly the artist of the family, and his paintings, and those of Catalan colleagues, line the walls, and are displayed in a small gallery; his studio is on the top floor. But Anna's artistry is plain in the interior design which is all highly individual (the brightly decorated breakfast room and hand-made bedspreads are a joy), and in the breakfasts, which are also something special.

Anna and Isdre serve no other meals, though they offer the occasional beer, and advise (at length) on where to eat in the town. Service is highly personal, but this is not a hotel. Rooms have few *en suite* facilities and visitors who demand to see them before checking in risk being turned away. Anna and Isdre are busy enough with their satisfied regulars, and do not advertise. Indeed, it took an hour of pleading over a beer to elicit the information we needed for an entry here.

Nearby Cathedral; museums; old Gerona.

Calle Bellmirall 3, 17000, Gerona
Tel (972) 204009
Location in tiny street next to cathedral; no private parking
Meals breakfast
Prices 2,268-6,048pts with breakfast
Rooms 3 double, 2 with shower; 2 single, one with shower; 2 family rooms, both with shower; all rooms have phone

Facilities sitting-room, breakfast room
Credit cards not accepted
Children welcome
Disabled no special facilities
Pets tolerated
Closed Jan and Feb
Proprietor Pascual Laromaine Anna

Gerona

Seaside hotel, Llansa, Gerona

Hotel Berna

There is nothing particularly remarkable about the Hotel Berna – informal, friendly and well run, but not notably full of character – except that it is situated at the quiet end of the marine parade in the relatively unspoiled harbour village of Llansa. And there are few places left on the Costas these days where you can walk off a bar terrace straight on to a sandy beach, without being drowned in bodies. Here you can, provided you avoid the very peak of the season.

The Berna is a renovated survivor from the first wave of tourism that hit the Costas thirty or so years ago. The utilitarian construction is hidden by climbing plants and partially faced with stone. Inside, some of the original features remain, but all is reasonably tasteful. We preferred the old blue-tiled bathrooms with white enamel basins to the more modern fittings with which they are gradually being replaced. The better rooms have a balcony with wicker tables and chairs where you can relax and enjoy the view. The only drawback of visiting out of high season is that the restaurant is closed, but it is still possible to enjoy a good breakfast on the terrace, shielded from the breeze by the thoughtful addition of glass.

Nearby Marine parade, market, harbour and beach.

Paseo Maritimo 13, 17490, Llansa, Gerona
Tel (972) 380150
Location on traffic-free promenade
Meals breakfast, lunch, dinner, snacks
Prices rooms 5,300-6,200pts; breakfast 500pts; meals 1,900pts
Rooms 36 double, all with bath and shower; 4 single, all with bath; all rooms have phone; most have balcony
Facilities dining-rooms, sitting-rooms, bar
Credit cards not accepted
Children welcome
Disabled access easy; some ground-floor rooms
Pets well behaved ones accepted
Closed Oct to May, except Easter; restaurant only Jun and Sep **Proprietor** Maria Teresa Campos

Gerona

Seaside hotel, Palafrugell

Hotel Casamar

This quiet, 1976 conversion of a small Catalan village house is pleasantly off the main thoroughfare without being isolated. The pretty, shaded terrace overlooks the promenade, and wide stone steps lead down to the beach. Inside, José Casellas keeps an eye on everything. Before you have finished the first meal (a generous three-course set menu that rotates on a 15-day cycle), language barriers have been overcome, and all are gently sharing a joke.

The cool dining-room is clearly the heart of the place. In high season it is reserved for guests, although José does allow favoured passers-by to wander in during quieter periods. Slightly dated modern furniture is much enhanced by the fresh flowers that top the crisp table settings. Bedrooms are comfortable, although nothing special, with some attention to those important little details such as mirrors and lights. Most have balconies with views to the sea or the mountains behind. All have safes.

After meals there is nothing for it but to relax on the terrace with a drink and watch the world go by. Behind you, a collection of plates, from places as diverse as Luzern and Cymru, are displayed on the wall – gifts from José's appreciative regulars.
Nearby Palafrugell (4 km); coastal walks; beach and harbour.

Nero 3, 17200, Palafrugell, Gerona
Tel (972) 300104
Location on cliffs at south end of town, with steps to beach and promenade; with car parking
Meals breakfast, lunch, dinner
Prices rooms 3,360-6,720pts; breakfast 500pts, lunch and dinner 1,700pts; discounts for children
Rooms 17 double, 5 with bath, 12 with shower; 3 single, 2 with bath, one with shower; all rooms have central heating, phone
Facilities dining-room, sitting-room/bar, terrace
Credit cards MC, V
Children welcome
Disabled access difficult
Pets tolerated
Closed 15 Oct to 1 Apr
Proprietor José Casellas Balaguer

Gerona

Seaside hotel, Palafrugell

Hotel Llevant

This unassuming three-storey house, right on the main promenade of the surprisingly unspoilt fishing village of Llafranc, was a restaurant before the Spanish Civil War. It had only six rooms when Jaume Farrarons took it over. Since then the family have built it up to its current 28 rooms, and now they feel enough is enough, though they are planning a few minor improvements. Food is their true love, and heaven forbid that the hotel should start to overshadow the restaurant.

For the time being, at least, they have no need to worry: the Llevant's individual French-influenced Catalan cuisine draws a discerning crowd at all times of year. The excellent fish dishes are much enhanced by the sea air and sophisticated French café-style surroundings. The four-course menu will leave you staggering for a comfortable chair, which you will find without difficulty on the covered terrace adjoining, or in the small salon where exhibitions of local art are regularly housed.

If you are not up to the similarly proportioned buffet breakfasts of cheese and charcuterie, then a simpler Continental breakfast can be taken in the bedrooms, which are simple but airy and tasteful.

Nearby Palafrugell (4 km); coastal walks; beach and harbour.

Francesc de Blanes 5, 17200, Palafrugell, Gerona
Tel (972) 300366
Location on main promenade in heart of village; no private car parking
Meals breakfast, lunch, dinner
Prices rooms 4,750-8,150pts; breakfast 625pts, dinner 1,500pts
Rooms 24 double, 14 with bath, 10 with shower; 4 single, with bath; all rooms have central heating; 10 rooms have air-conditioning, 8 rooms have TV
Facilities dining-room, sitting-room, bar, terrace
Credit cards not accepted
Children welcome
Disabled access difficult
Pets accepted in rooms
Closed Nov to 15 Dec; restaurant only, Sun night Jan to Mar
Proprietor Jaume Farrarons

Gerona

Seaside hotel, Palafrugell

Hotel Sant Roc

High on the cliffs of Calella de Palafrugell, with magnificent views from the leafy terrace over the bay and steps down to the shore, the Sant Roc started life as a family home in the 1950s but was soon converted to an hotel, and has been expanded since. It is an appealing building, in style somewhere between a grand Catalan country house and a mini-monastery, featuring a terracota roofed tower.

It aims to be a family-run hotel run for families. Señor Salada finds time to mix his guests' cocktails personally, likes to practise his English, and stubbornly resists expansion on the part of the well-known tour operator who fills a quarter of his beds in summer, for fear it would upset the atmosphere.

The interior is stylish, but lived in. The wicker rocking chairs and antiques are there to be used, as is the more utilitarian furniture. You might find the wallpaper peeling in those rooms that are next on the list for re-furbishment, and not all have sea views, but they are all clean with traditional Catalan wooden furniture painted in red, green or blue, known as polycromodo.

The three-course dinner and lunch menu has three choices for starter and main-course, and there is always the *carte*.

Nearby Calella (1.5 km); Palafrugell (4 km); beach.

Calella de Palafrugell, 17210, Palafrugell, Gerona
Tel (972) 300500
Location on cliffs, set back from road amid trees; with garden and car parking
Meals breakfast, lunch, dinner
Prices rooms 5,300-8,200pts; FB 7,000pts; breakfast 550pts, dinner 1,600pts
Rooms 38 double, 22 with bath, 16 with shower; 5 single, 3 with shower; 9 family rooms,
6 with bath, 3 with shower; all have central heating, phone
Facilities dining-room, sitting-room, bar, terrace; table tennis
Credit cards AE, DC, MC, V
Children welcome; baby-sitting available
Disabled lift/elevator; ground-floor rooms
Pets accepted in rooms
Closed Nov to Mar
Manager Teresa Boix Salada

Gerona

Seaside hotel, S'Agaró

Hostal de la Gavina

Set in secluded grounds on the edge of S'Agaró, above a small beach (with brightly painted huts, straight out of a 1930s musical, where the rich and famous rub sun-burnt shoulders with the merely affluent), this majestic Catalan villa is reminiscent of the great palaces of Europe, except that it is better cared for. A full description of the furnishings would read like a Christie's catalogue; as you wander through the circular formation of marbled salons and halls, the eye is met by enticing clusters of antique furniture, making it impossible to decide whether to continue or sit down. The immaculate bedrooms are all individually furnished in the style of your choice – Regency, rich walnut, Catalan polycromodo ...

Not all is elegance. The 'El Barco' bar is, as its name suggests, built like the inside of a wooden boat. There are two restaurants, both serving the same decadent French/Spanish *carte* – one in French brasserie style, the other candle-lit, in plush Regency style, jacket and tie required.

Run by the son of the man who built it, the place is surprisingly relaxed for somewhere so opulent. The only thing keeping most people away is the price.

Nearby Sant Feliu de Guíxols (4 km); beach.

Plaza de la Rosaleda, 17248, S'Agaró, Gerona
Tel (972) 321100
Location above beach on edge of main S'Agaró development; with gardens, and garaging for 14 cars and car parking
Meals breakfast, lunch, dinner
Prices rooms 21,500-30,000pts; breakfast 1,450pts, menus 4,700pts
Rooms 56 double, 2 single, 16 suites, all with bath; all rooms have phone, TV, radio, minibar, hairdrier
Facilities 2 dining-rooms, sitting-rooms, bar, gymnasium, sauna, jacuzzi, terrace; sea-water pool, tennis courts
Credit cards AE, DC, MC, V
Children accepted
Disabled access easy; ground-floor rooms; lift/elevator **Pets** accepted in bedrooms **Closed** Nov to Mar
Manager Gustavo Jean-Mairet

Gerona

Seaside hotel, Tamariú

Hotel Hostalillo

This modern hotel is lifted out of the Costa rut by attention to detail and its tranquil location. Some credit must go to Carlos Xargay, the hotel's director, who (despite the fact that we try not to over-use this adjective) can really only be described as charming. His staff are efficient and helpful, the atmosphere welcoming – the hotel feels much smaller than its rule-breaking 72 rooms. Even from the outside, it is more than usually appealing: the five storeys are set into the steep hillside and pitched terracotta roofs break up the lines of the concrete.

The white walls inside give a cool, airy feel. The large split-level dining room is flexible enough not to seem bare, even in low season. Here the four-course menu (constantly varied, plenty of choice) can be struggled through, overlooking the inviting sun terrace full of geraniums and simple, comfortable chairs. Below is the once-picturesque fishing village of Tamariú, where the boats on the beach still out-number the frying bodies except in July and August. Steps lead through the garden, down the cliffs to the beach.

Bedrooms have all you can expect from a sound, basic beach hotel, including a view of the bay or the mountains.

Nearby Palafrugell (4 km); coastal walks; beach.

Bellavista 22, 17212, Tamariú, Gerona
Tel (972) 300158
Location on cliffs above village, overlooking Tamariú; with garden and parking for 13 cars
Meals breakfast, lunch, dinner
Prices rooms 10,000-12,000pts; breakfast 550pts, menus 2,000pts
Rooms 59 double, 11 single, 3 family rooms, all with bath; all rooms have phone; most rooms have central heating
Facilities dining-room, sitting/TV room
Credit cards V
Children accepted
Disabled access difficult
Pets not accepted
Closed 24 Sep to 1 Jun
Manager Carlos Xargay

Gerona

Country hotel, Viladrau

Hostal de la Glòria

This cosy country lodge was built 50 years ago in simple Catalan style. Set just above the pleasant mountain village of Viladrau, with a pretty, peaceful garden terrace in front and the Sierra rising behind, it is a favourite with ageing Spanish card-players, who fill the inter-connecting small salons and leatherette arm-chairs at weekends throughout the year.

The Formatje family have decked the place out with copper pots, brass lamps, paintings and some fine old Spanish chairs, and keep the whole spotlessly clean. They are proud of their hostal, always eager to please, and genuinely apologetic when their rooms are full.

Rooms are simple and old-fashioned, with modern bathrooms. The four-course lunch and dinner menus are different each day, and are highly recommended. They are served in an attractive arched dining-room with a pretty tiled floor, wooden beams, green lace curtains and white walls hand-painted with birds and decorated with plates.

Overall, the result is an unpretentious home from home, where relaxation comes naturally – aided by the knowledge that rooms and meals are notably cheap.

Nearby Gerona (60 km); Vich (25 km); Montseny Sierra.

Torreventosa 12, 08553, Viladrau, Gerona
Tel (93) 884 9034
Location above mountain village in Sierra de Montseny; with covered car park
Meals breakfast, lunch, dinner
Prices rooms 2,500-4,500pts; breakfast 450pts, dinner 1,650pts
Rooms 24 double, 4 single , all with bath; all rooms have central heating, phone, TV

Facilities dining-room, sitting-room, bar
Credit cards V
Children accepted
Disabled no special facilities
Pets not accepted
Closed Oct
Proprietors Formatje family

Gerona

Country hotel, Figueras

Mas Pau

This creeper-covered family-run hotel is a converted 17thC *masia* (a large, well-to-do farmhouse) standing by itself in wooded and farmed countryside near the village of Figueras (made famous by Salvador Dali). It has been run by Nuria Serrat and her family for over fifteen years and, wedding parties permitting, you can be certain of friendly personal service.

The public rooms are essentially rustic, but decorated in *modernista* style, the Spanish equivalent of *art nouveau*. They include an arched bar (with painted mirrors, vases of ferns, wicker chairs around tables made from old sewing machines), and three interconnecting dining-rooms. The largest of these, the banqueting room, has a beamed ceiling and stone walls covered in old photos of Figueras. The seven modern bedrooms (including one suite) look out on to tranquil gardens and cypress trees. They are decorated entirely in pink and grey; grey carpets, pink marble bathrooms and – according to Señora Serrat – curtains and bedspreads that change with the seasons: warm pink in winter, cool grey in summer.

In the well established gardens is a modest but attractive pool, with a shaded terrace on hand.

Nearby Figueras – Dali museum; Gerona (40 km).

Avinyonet de Puigventós, 17742, Figueras, Gerona
Tel (972) 546154
Location in countryside, 4 km SW of village of Figueras; with garden and car parking
Meals breakfast, lunch, dinner
Prices rooms 12,000-18,000pts; breakfast 1,200pts; meals from 2,780pts
Rooms 6 double, one suite, all with bath; all rooms have central heating, phone, TV, air-conditioning, minibar
Facilities dining-room, sitting-room, banquet/conference room, terrace; swimming-pool
Credit cards AE, DC, MC, V
Children welcome; playground
Disabled easy access; some ground-floor rooms
Pets dogs accepted
Closed Jan and Feb; restaurant only, Sun in winter
Proprietor Nuria Serrat Bofill

Gerona

Country house hotel, Torrent

Hotel Mas de Torrent

The setting of this stunning recent conversion of a 1751 Catalan *masia* is truly superb: in lush grounds concealing extensive terraces, pelota, paddleball and tennis courts, and the inevitable swimming-pool, amid open countryside, with views over Pals to the castle at Bagur beyond.

Just when you have come to terms with the exterior, you are confronted by further splendour inside. The style of the original interior is faithfully reproduced, but with a layer of luxury applied with impeccable taste. A series of arched salons with bright sofas and a fireplace gives way to the bar and terraces. Upstairs there are further spacious salons, with huge sofas and antiques, around which the individually named and styled rooms are set. 'Las Hortensias' is all antiques and lace, for example, while 'Las Dacias' is pure Barcelona chic. The 20 rooms in the garden bungalows have private, hedged terraces and more of a summerhouse feel. All are faultless in terms of facilities.

The dining-room which adjoins the main building is an impressive reproduction, with the exposed roof beams and slates typical of the region. There is an extravagant four-course menu and seasonal *carte* of Catalan, Basque and French cuisine.

Nearby Pals (4 km); Costa Brava beaches (14 km).

17123, Torrent, Gerona
Tel (972) 303292
Location in open countryside near tiny village; with garden and car parking
Meals breakfast, lunch, dinner
Prices rooms 20,000-28,000pts; breakfast 1,300pts, dinner 5,500pts
Rooms 30 double, all with bath; all rooms have central heating, air-conditioning, phone, TV, minibar, radio, hairdrier
Facilities dining-room, 4 sitting-rooms, games room; swimming-pool, tennis court
Credit cards AE, DC, MC, V
Children accepted; games room
Disabled access easy; specially adapted room and other ground-floor rooms
Pets accepted in bedrooms
Closed never
Manager Alejandro Figueras

Zamora

Castle Parador, Benavente

PN Rey Fernando II de León

One look at the extraordinary sitting-room and you will probably
excuse whatever shortcomings this hotel has. This voluminous
hall occupies most of the old castle keep, the Tower of the Snail
(the only part of the original building which was not destroyed
by the French in the last century), which stands on a prominent
cliff a short way out of town. Deep corner alcoves penetrate the
turrets to reach snug stone benches by sunny windows. Large old
tapestries adorn the walls. Overhead is a magnificent Mudejar
coffered ceiling which was taken from a church.

A worn stone staircase (straight out of *The Name of the Rose*)
takes you to another striking chamber below – the second bar,
open only in the evenings – which has 2-metre thick walls, an
enormous circular iron chandelier and some extremely interesting old furnishings.

The rest of the hotel, however, is modern and characterless in
comparison. The dining-room and smaller bar have brick arches
and a wall of windows giving views of fertile agricultural plains
(shame about the flour mill immediately below). Twenty of the
rooms have balconies sharing the same view.

Nearby Zamora (65 km); León (69 km); Puebla de Sanabria (84
km).

Parque de la Marina
Española, 49600, Benavente,
Zamora
Tel (988) 630300
Location on hill overlooking
town; with garden and car
parking
Meals breakfast, lunch, dinner
Prices rooms 8,000-10,500pts;
breakfast 1,100pts, dinner
3,200pts
Rooms 28 double, 2 single, all
with bath; all rooms have

central heating,
air-conditioning, phone, TV,
minibar
Facilities dining-room,
sitting-room, 2 bars, TV room
Credit cards AE, DC, MC, V
Children welcome
Disabled access easy; 9
ground-floor rooms
Pets not accepted
Closed never
Manager Concepción
Lechuga Arribas

Zamora

Hotel Juan II

Named after one of the many royals that distinguish the history of Toro, Hotel Juan II is worth an overnight stop for its panoramic view alone. Ten of the bedrooms have large terraces looking over the River Duero and the surrounding plains from a cliff-top vantage point. The rooms in general are, though sparsely furnished, without much character. The hotel has little public space in which to relax, but the smaller of the two dining-rooms, the 'Castilian' one, is dark and intimate with a sloping beamed roof. Don't bother asking for the sitting-room.

Nearby Toro Collegiate Church (across the square); Zamora (30 km); San Pedro de la Nave, Visigothic Church (50 km).

paseo del Espolón, 49800, Toro, Zamora
Tel (988) 690300
Location in square behind church; with car parking
Meals breakfast, lunch, dinner
Prices rooms 2,450-4500pts; breakfast 290pts, menu 900pts
Rooms 34 double, 8 single, all with bath; all rooms have central heating, phone; most rooms have TV

Facilities sitting-room, dining-room, bar, terrace; swimming-pool
Credit cards AE, DC, MC, V
Children welcome
Disabled access easy; lift available
Pets not accepted
Closed never
Manager Rosa Maria Piorno Carral

Paradores in Western Spain

The provinces of Zamora and Salamanca (around the NE corner of Portugal) have several pleasant Paradores which are described in detail in this section. In addition, Salamanca's modern white Parador sits on a hill above the town, traditionally the site of one of Castille's biggest cattle fairs. The best we can say about the hotel is that every guest room has a superb view of the town at night. Rooms are adequate and have sliding doors leading to small 'galleries' furnished with cane chairs (Tel (923) 268700).

The further south you travel, the fewer and further between Paradores become. The harsh terrain of Extremadura has kept the developers out from Roman times onwards, and only recently (and with a lot of funding from the EC, drawn to your attention on huge billboards at regular intervals) has the area been opened up by an extensive network of new roads. The existing Paradores, now more accessible, are all in ancient buildings – converted monasteries (Trujillo, Guadalupe, Mérida), hilltop castles (Oropesa, Jarandilla, Zafra) and a 14thC town house at Cáceres. Most have detailed entries. But when we visited two potentially splendid castles – the imposing 15thC PN Hernán Cortés in the middle of Zafra (Tel (924) 550200) and the PN Virrey de Toledo, perched above the little town of Oropesa (Tel (925) 430000) – were closed for extensive renovations.

Zamora

Palace Parador, Zamora

PN Condes de Alba y Aliste

Zamora may seem out of the way for most visitors, but here is a hotel worth the detour. Much less interfered with than other Paradors occupying historic buildings, this palace surrounds a photogenic Renaissance courtyard fringed with carved stone pillars. The sunny enclosed halls and balconies along the four sides of the courtyard are decorated with antiques and pot plants (there are even plants sprouting out of an antique chest).

Many of the furnishings are original, or at least apt; the tarnished-green dining-room chandeliers have stags fleeing from their hubs. And at the foot of the stairs a complete suit of armour for a knight and his horse is on display. Most of the bedrooms also have an old-fashioned feel; that is, they don't feel anonymously modern. Some of them have double-doored windows opening on to the swimming-pool. Two rooms have canopied double beds, while the two suites available are as large as apartments.

The swimming-pool is open to the public, making this Parador feel less privileged than most others, particularly at weekends, when the pool can be busy (and noisy).

Nearby Romanesque churches; Gothic altarpiece, Arcenillas (6 km); 7thC Visigothic church, near El Campillo (20 km).

plaza Viriato 5, 49001, Zamora
Tel (988) 514497
Location in main square; with garden and car parking
Meals breakfast, lunch, dinner
Prices rooms 11,000-12,000pts; breakfast 1,100pts, dinner 3,200pts
Rooms 25 doubles, 2 suites, all with bath; all rooms have central heating, phone, TV, minibar
Facilities dining-room, 2 sitting-rooms, bar, terrace; swimming-pool (public)
Credit cards AE, DC, MC, V
Children welcome
Disabled easy access; lift/elevator
Pets accepted
Closed never
Manager Pilar Pelegrin Gracia

92

Zamora

Modern Parador, Puebla de Sanabria

PN de Puebla de Sanabria

This is a rather dull modern Parador, but it is built at a strategic point off the Madrid to Orense road, sandwiched between the Portugese border and the foothills of the Sierra de la Cabrera. There is some spectacular scenery in these mountains, and the Lake of Sanabria, some 15 km north of the Parador, is set in a National Park of great beauty which offers hiking, watersports and wildlife reserves.

The cuisine of this region reflects the fruits of these rivers and forests: trout and salmon as well as game dishes feature on the Parador menus as the seasons allow.

The Parador building itself is whitewashed, with stone features reflecting local traditions, and inside there is a distinctive simplicity which is easy on the eye: a plain granite fireplace in the sitting-room, dark stone floor in the dining-room and polished marble in the hallways. As you walk through Puebla de Sanabria you will see this same pattern in the buildings of the town, which is capped by the remains of a solid 15thC castle, part of the massive defences against Portugal built during the long-running wars between the two countries.

Nearby Lake of Sanabria (15 km); San Martín de Castañeda – Romanesque church with fabulous views (15 km).

49300, Puebla de Sanabria, Zamora
Tel (988) 620001
Location in suburban area on outskirts of town; with ample shaded car parking
Meals breakfast, lunch, dinner
Prices rooms 7,000-8,500pts; breakfast 1,000pts; meals 3,000pts
Rooms 32 double, 5 single, 7 suites, all with bath; all rooms have central heating, phone, TV
Facilities dining-room, sitting-room, bar, lobby, 2 conference rooms
Credit cards AE, DC, MC, V
Children accepted
Disabled some ground-floor rooms; lift/elevator
Pets not accepted
Closed never
Manager Marcelo Pascual Gutierrez

Salamanca

Hotel Conde Rodrigo

The Conde Rodrigo occupies a handsome 16thC stone-built palace on a leafy, historic square. It has, unfortunately, been insensitively modernized inside, obviously with the best of intentions. The bedrooms, though adequate, lack character but they offer some surprise extras, such as shoe-brushes in the bathrooms. It is popular for family functions, when the sitting-room is converted into a rowdy banqueting hall. There is also a disco in the basement. The restaurant serves a varied and economical menu. A sister hotel, Conde Rodrigo II, just out of town, is unashamedly modern, with its own pool and tennis court.
Nearby Plaza Mayor (short walk); Portugal (30 km).

plaza de San Salvador 9, 37500, Ciudad Rodrigo, Salamanca
Tel (923) 461404
Location in square in historic centre, signed from Salamanca road; with small car parking area
Meals breakfast, lunch, dinner
Prices rooms 3,550-5,400pts; breakfast 350pts, menu 1,300pts

Rooms 31 double with bath, 4 single with shower; all rooms have central heating, phone, TV, minibar, radio
Facilities sitting-room, dining-room, bar, terrace, disco
Credit cards AE, DC, MC, V
Children Welcome
Disabled access easy
Pets not accepted
Closed never
Manager Ceferino Santos

Las Batuecas

A popular weekend destination for Madrileños, Las Batuecas is an imposing stone building located on the edge of the quaint village of La Alberca, in the heart of the fascinating Sierra de Francia, with its chestnut-woods and picturesque terraces of cherry-trees. The hotel begins on the first floor with a wide, covered terrace. Behind is a garden with a lawn and rose-clad trellis, and the rest of the floor is an open-plan lounge-bar-dining-room. Don't expect more than a basic bedroom – although the manager has plans to renovate all the bathrooms. A useful base for walking, cycling or touring.
Nearby La Alberca; Las Batuecas scenic road (40 km trip).

carretera Las Batuecas, 37624, La Alberca, Salamanca
Tel (923) 437030
Location in village; with garden and car parking
Meals breakfast, lunch, dinner
Prices rooms 5,000-5,500pts; breakfast 375pts, lunch 1,350pts, dinner 1,050pts
Rooms 19 double, 2 single, 3 family rooms, all with bath; all rooms have central heating,

phone
Facilities sitting-room, dining-room, bar, terrace
Credit cards MC, V
Children welcome
Disabled access difficult
Pets accepted only in bedrooms
Closed never
Manager Manuel Hernandez Perez

Salamanca

Castle Parador, Ciudad Rodrigo

PN Enrique II

Don't be disappointed if what you thought was the hotel – a stout tower with battlements – turns out to be only a warehouse. The hotel itself is the low-lying, attractively ivy-clad building beneath it.

This was the second Parador to be opened, and the first to occupy a historic building. Fortunately, the present manager has paid more personal attention to it than many of those running other castles in the state hotel chain.

The rooms are spread out along two wings – one ancient, one modern. The former are reached by an arched curving white corridor; the 'star' is Room 10, a suite in which the bedroom is circular with a domed roof. Four of the new rooms abut the old city walls and have views over the hotel's formal gardens.

The public areas are decorated with occasional antiques, some suits of armour and plenty of green pot plants. The dining-room and sitting-room are both attractive, with partially sloping ceilings and wide basket-handle stone arches.

For pure history and a great view, don't forget to climb the tower. It is reached through the castle's original gate (ask for the key from reception), now in a splendid, crumbling state.

Nearby Plaza Mayor; Portugal (30 km); La Alberca (50 km).

plaza del Castillo 1, 37500, Ciudad Rodrigo, Salamanca
Tel (923) 460150
Location on a quiet open square near centre of town; with garden and car parking
Meals breakfast, lunch, dinner
Prices rooms 8,000-11,000pts; breakfast 1,100pts, dinner 3,200pts
Rooms 26 double, 1 suite, all with bath; all rooms have central heating, phone, TV, minibar
Facilities dining-room, 2 sitting-rooms, bar, patio
Credit cards AE, DC, MC, V
Children welcome; 20% discount for children under 10
Disabled access difficult
Pets not accepted
Closed never
Manager Angel Aliste Lopez

Cáceres

Converted hospice, Guadalupe

PN Zurbarán

Named after the 17thC painter, this Parador started life as a hospice in the 14thC, housing pilgrims who had come to venerate the Black Virgin of Guadalupe. The road through the hills has probably not improved much since their day, but the spectacular views of mountains and valleys – and of Guadalupe – make up for the hairpin bends and pot-holes.

The Parador is a simple, whitewashed building, centred around an open cobbled courtyard full of orange trees, with dozens of peculiar domed chimney-pots on its red-tiled roofs. Low arched doorways in the cloisters lead to a sitting-room on one side and a wood-beamed bar on the other. The dining-room, on the third side of the quadrangle, looks out through French windows on to lovely gardens. In summer, tables are set on the terrace, so you can eat and drink overlooking a water-garden and tiled pavilion beyond.

The modern concrete annexe of twenty bedrooms overlooks the gardens and swimming pool. Rooms here are more spacious than those in the old part and all have balconies. But they do lack character, and it is always the original rooms that sell out.

Nearby 14thC Franciscan monastery (Zurbarán's paintings), mountain passes and surrounding countryside.

Marqués de la Romana 10, 10140, Guadalupe, Cáceres
Tel (927) 367075
Location opposite Franciscan Monastery, in middle of town; with garden and garage
Meals breakfast, lunch, dinner
Prices rooms 7,000-11,000pts; breakfast 1,100pts, dinner 3,200pts
Rooms 40 double, all with bath; all rooms have central heating, phone, TV, minibar, radio; most rooms have air-conditioning
Facilities 2 dining-rooms, sitting-room, bar; swimming-pool, tennis court
Credit cards AE, DC, MC, V
Children welcome
Disabled ground-floor rooms; lift/elevator
Pets accepted but not in dining-room
Closed never
Manager Manuel Arias Ariai

Cáceres

Converted monastery, Guadalupe

Hospedería del Real Monasterio

The Hospedería is part of a 16thC monastery, which dominates the Guadalupe skyline. It is still a working monastery; Franciscan brothers live in one half of the building, guests in the other.

The bedrooms are set around a magnificent stone-arcaded courtyard. Many of them are the original monks' cells – long narrow rooms with high ceilings and low stone doorways. They are all different; some very elaborate, some very basic. On one side there is an exquisite suite full of ornate antiques, on the other, simple single rooms.

The public rooms downstairs are equally original; the sombre sitting-room contrasts with a cheerful white dining-room, with fresh flowers on every table. There is also a TV room set out like a cinema, and an inviting bar with an arched roof and marble floor. Tables are set out in the courtyard among terracotta pots of geraniums and entwined giant cacti.

Although we arrived in the middle of a wedding reception for two hundred guests, the staff were not remotely put out and could not have been more helpful – the monks even gave us a guided tour of the monastery.

Nearby 14thC Franciscan monastery (Zurbarán's paintings); mountain passes and surrounding countryside.

Plaza Juan Carlos 1, 10140, Guadalupe, Cáceres
Tel (927) 367000
Location within monastery, entrance up a flight of steps from main road; parking for 30 cars
Meals breakfast, lunch, dinner
Prices rooms 3,800-5,800pts; breakfast 500pts, dinner 2,100pts
Rooms 22 double, one single, 17 family rooms, all with bath; all rooms have central heating, phone; some rooms have air-conditioning
Facilities dining-room, sitting-room, TV room, bar
Credit cards MC, V
Children welcome
Disabled ground-floor rooms, lift/elevator
Pets not accepted
Closed Jan 15 to Feb 15
Proprietor Franciscan brothers

Cáceres

Converted castle, Jarandilla de la Vera

PN Carlos V

An imposing 15thC castle on the edge of a little white town makes a perfect setting for a Parador – which is why the Carlos V is often fully booked. The Parador architects have modernized it without losing any of its medieval flavour; it is difficult to tell that the new extension is not part of the original building. An arched doorway between round towers leads into a cobbled courtyard. Small shuttered windows peep out of cold grey walls and an arcaded balcony looks down from solid square towers.

Most of the public rooms are simply furnished in a modern style. Sombre oil paintings hang on the walls of the upstairs sitting-room, which opens on to the balcony set with yellow and white chairs. The bar and dining-room are bright and comfortable, and look on to the Parador gardens. The original bedrooms lead off tall, narrow, beamed corridors and have all the usual facilities. Rooms in the extension are light and spacious.

There is plenty to do outside; for the energetic, a swimming-pool and tennis court; for children, a play area with swings and slides; and for those who just want to relax, lovely rose gardens surrounding this historic castle.

Nearby Yuste monastery (10 km); Trujillo, Cáceres, Avila, within driving distance.

Carretera de Plascencia, 10450, Jarandilla de la Vera, Cáceres
Tel (927) 560117
Location at top of town, on a rock with gardens around it; with car parking
Meals breakfast, lunch, dinner
Prices rooms 9,000-12,000pts; breakfast 1,100pts, dinner 3,200pts
Rooms 53 double, all with bath; all rooms have central heating, air-conditioning, phone, TV, minibar
Facilities 2 dining-rooms, 3 sitting-rooms, bar; swimming-pool, tennis court
Credit cards AE, DC, MC, V
Children welcome
Disabled ground-floor rooms
Pets not accepted
Closed never
Manager Miguel Fages Argente

Cáceres

Town house, Trujillo

Mesón La Cadena

A smaller, cheaper alternative to the Trujillo Parador is the
Mesón La Cadena, on the main square. It is really a restaurant
(and noisy bar) with rooms, rather than a hotel, but it merits
inclusion because of its central location and views over the
square – a great place for watching the world go by from tables
set out on the cobbled street.

The bedrooms are all on the third floor of this attractive
granite house, far enough away from the noisy bar to be assured
of a good night's sleep. They are simple and charming, with dark
wooden furniture and brightly coloured rugs, woven locally.
Rooms at the back have sloping ceilings, and look out on to the
hill leading up to the castle.

One floor below is the restaurant, on three sides of a tiny
internal courtyard, decorated with wrought iron lamps and local
pottery plates on white walls. It is a lively place in the evenings,
offering an interesting daily menu at a very reasonable price.
The food is simple and good, and the waiters are friendly. The
bar on the ground floor is also a popular spot and a good place
to meet the locals.

Nearby Castle, palaces of the Conquistadors, old city walls.

Plaza Mayor 8, 10200, Trujillo,
Cáceres
Tel (927) 321463
Location on main square in
middle of town; car parking in
square
Meals breakfast, lunch, dinner
Prices rooms 4,000pts;
breakfast 150pts, dinner
1,000-1,500pts
Rooms 8 double, all with bath;
all rooms have central
heating, air-conditioning

Facilities 2 dining-rooms,
sitting-room, bar
Credit cards not accepted
Children welcome
Disabled access difficult
Pets not accepted
Closed never
Manager Juan Vicente
Mariscal Mayordomo

Cáceres

PN de Trujillo

Built in 1984 in the 16thC convent of Santa Clara, this is the newest and one of the loveliest of Spain's Paradores. The setting is perfect – it is away from Trujillo's busy main square, in a maze of quiet, narrow streets overlooking the plains of Extremadura, yet within easy walking distance of all the palaces and churches.

Some of the rooms are set in the old part of the convent, around a pretty courtyard full of orange and lemon trees. The cloisters lead off to a magnificent arched refectory through an ancient wooden door. This is now used as a bar and sitting area – a somewhat austere setting for writing postcards. The public rooms have been decorated with the convent in mind – furniture is simple, paintings are religious, and wooden crosses hang over the arches in the cloisters.

Half the bedrooms are in the nuns' old quarters, reached through low arched doorways from the gallery around the court-yard. The rest are in an adjoining modern building around a second courtyard which encloses an inviting hexagonal swimming-pool. Book early – this Parador is extremely popular (visit, and you will soon understand why).

Nearby castle, palaces of the Conquistadors, churches, old city walls and gates; Cáceres (50 km); Guadalupe (80 km).

Plaza de Santa Clara, 10200, Trujillo, Cáceres
Tel (927) 321350
Location on hill in narrow streets just outside town centre; with car parking and garage
Meals breakfast, lunch, dinner
Prices rooms 9,000-13,000pts; breakfast 1,100pts, dinner 3,200pts
Rooms 45 double, one family room, all with bath; all rooms have central heating, air-conditioning, phone, TV, minibar, hairdrier
Facilities 2 dining-rooms, 2 sitting-rooms with TV; swimming-pool
Credit cards AE, DC, MC, V
Children accepted
Disabled ground-floor rooms
Pets not accepted
Closed never
Manager José Rizos Garrido

Badajoz

Town mansion hotel, Mérida

Hotel Emperatriz

Mérida is a lively historic town, although now (thanks to Moorish plundering of its stone) no more than half the size that it was in Roman times. The Emperatriz stands at its heart – a 16thC mansion, built of sandy-coloured granite in a privileged position on the main square.

The rather unprepossessing entrance opens into a grand cloistered courtyard, surrounded by granite pillars and arches on two floors. When we visited, dining-tables were laid in the courtyard for a wedding banquet – the effect was spectacular. The usual place to dine is an arched room off the cloisters, divided in two by elaborate wrought iron grilles. There are also two public bars, both underground, one serving *tapas*.

The hotel does not have all the facilities you expect in a Parador, but it has the character and sense of history that many of them lack. The bedrooms are all irregular shapes but are similarly furnished – embroidered bedspreads, wooden furniture and large bathrooms. Those with little balconies, facing on to the busy square full of outdoor cafés and ice-cream stalls, are rather noisy, at least by day.

Nearby Roman theatre, arena and villa, Alcazaba; Badajoz (60 km), Zafra (65 km), Cáceres (70 km), Trujillo (90 km).

Plaza de España 19, 06800, Mérida, Badajoz
Tel (924) 313111
Location on main square (follow signs to town centre); no private car parking
Meals breakfast, lunch, dinner
Prices rooms 6,000-6,780pts; breakfast 375pts, dinner 1,500pts
Rooms 17 double, 24 single, one family room, all with bath; all rooms have central heating, phone
Facilities dining-room, TV room, 2 bars
Credit cards V
Children welcome
Disabled no special facilities
Pets welcome
Closed never
Manager Manuel Rodriguez Nieto

Badajoz

Historic building, Mérida

PN Vía de la Plata

Mérida's chequered history is reflected in almost every room of the Parador Vía de la Plata (named after the Roman road it was built on). Roman friezes, acanthus capitals and ceramic urns come from the Augustan temple and Praetorian palace that stood here in Roman times. Visigothic stones and columns are evidence of a governor's residence, while Arabic inscriptions and decorations reveal later Moorish occupation. In the 16th century the Military Order of Santiago rebuilt the ruins as a monastery and their chapel now makes a stunning lounge. Although much of the Parador is modern, it is difficult not to get caught up in its intriguing web of history.

It stands on a quiet shady square, a short walk from the heart of town. Reception opens on to a pretty, typically Andalucian courtyard and a passage-way leads through to Moorish gardens. Most bedrooms look over the gardens, and are pleasant and spacious, with large marble bathrooms. Endless corridors lead to public rooms – a high-ceilinged sitting-room contrasting with a low beamed bar. All were busy when our inspectors visited, especially the dining-room, serving mouth-watering meals.

Nearby Roman theatre, arena and villa, Alcazaba; Badajoz (60 km), Zafra (65 km), Cáceres (70 km), Trujillo (90 km).

Plaza de la Constitución 3, 06800, Mérida, Badajoz
Tel (924) 313800
Location on quiet grassy square, in middle of old town; with garden and car parking
Meals breakfast, lunch, dinner
Prices rooms 13,000-15,000pts; breakfast 1,200pts, dinner 3,500pts
Rooms 79 double, one single, 2 family rooms; all rooms have central heating, air-conditioning, phone, TV, minibar, radio
Facilities 3 dining-rooms, 5 sitting-rooms, 2 bars
Credit cards AE, DC, MC, V
Children welcome
Disabled lift/elevator
Pets not accepted
Closed never
Manager Juan Carlos Morales Laveria

Badajoz

Hotel Huerta Honda

When our inspectors visited Zafra, the castle Parador was surrounded by scaffolding and in the throes of extensive redecoration. So they were delighted to discover, right next door, the Huerta Honda. This white villa, with red-tiled roofs and window-boxes dripping with geraniums, has fine views of the medieval castle. It is not merely a decent substitute for the Parador; in many ways, it is more attractive.

The hotel is built around a swimming-pool – the bedrooms on three sides, the dining-room on the fourth. Chairs and tables spill out of the bar and sitting-room around the pool, and it is a perfect place to enjoy a drink, between potted plants and trailing ivy. If you have had too much sun, you will appreciate the cool sitting-room, full of wicker furniture and wonderful ornaments (look out for the wicker pig under the mini grand piano, and the boar's head over the open fire). The dining-room is a similar haven, and the *menu del dia* excellent value. The hotel bar is a popular night spot and positively buzzes with activity. In contrast the bedrooms are serene; decorated in pastel shades with every possible comfort. You can be sure of a good night's sleep and of waking to a great view.

Nearby Llerena (40 km), Aracena (90 km).

Av López Azme 36, 06300, Zafra, Badajoz
Tel (924) 554100
Location next to castle Parador in heart of town; with car parking
Meals breakfast, lunch, dinner
Prices rooms 5,500-9,900pts; breakfast 750pts; meals 3,500pts
Rooms 40 double, 29 with bath, 11 with shower; 9 single with shower; 2 family rooms with bath; all have central heating, air- conditioning, phone, TV, minibar, radio, hairdrier **Facilities** dining-room, 2 sitting-rooms, 3 bars, terrace; swimming-pool **Credit cards** AE, DC, MC, V **Children** accepted **Disabled** access easy; ground- floor rooms; lift/elevator **Pets** accepted **Closed** never **Manager** Antonio Martinez Buzo

Segovia

City hotel, Segovia

Las Sirenas

Built in the 1950s as Segovia's 'grand hotel', Las Sirenas has never quite made it to the top but fails gloriously in the attempt. (You will still find most of the interior glass doors ostentatiously etched 'GHLS' – Grand Hotel Las Sirenas.) The whole place is attractively faded and tarnished, and full of life, making Segovia's might-have-been far more appealing than many of the city's more modern and expensive lodgings.

You will probably spend most of your time padding down long corridors, finding out where everything is. The building, with its long, wide entrance hall dotted with armchairs, pot plants and the odd grandfather clock, and its ceremonial staircase with padded handrail, includes a smoke-filled gentleman's club (or 'casino' as it is known), a cinema and a barber's shop. The sitting-room has a pleasant terrace bordered by wooden banisters: a quiet corner for breakfast.

The bedrooms, simple but elegant – often with parquet floors, polished mahogany furniture, substantial beds and new bathrooms – recall scenes from 1950s films. They are comfortable but not luxurious, and have a poor choice of lighting. Most are double glazed to keep out both the cold and noise.

Nearby Alcázar and aqueduct; La Granja (10 km).

Juan Bravo 30, 40001, Segovia
Tel (911) 434011
Location on square of same name, in front of church of San Martin; with car parking
Meals breakfast
Prices rooms 4,500-9,500pts; breakfast 350pts
Rooms 24 double, all with bath; 9 single, 6 with bath, 3 with shower; 3 suites, 3 family rooms, all with bath; all rooms have central heating,

air-conditioning, phone
Facilities sitting-room, bar, games room, terrace
Credit cards AE, DC, MC, V
Children welcome
Disabled access easy; lift/elevator
Pets not accepted
Closed never
Manager Jesus Escudero Alvarez

Segovia

Los Linajes

Behind its 11thC, half-timbered red-brick façade, this hotel is deceptively large and modern, stepping down the hillside beside the city wall in eight levels. The only part of the interior with any historical character is the reception area on the 3rd floor, which includes an enclosed courtyard and a pleasant seating-area where two wooden settles face each other beside an imitation fireplace. The basement lounge bar and terrace are dull by comparison. The rooms are functional and impersonal, but are saved by their comfortable blue-tiled bathrooms. The higher up the building, of course, the better the view.

Nearby Alcázar and aqueduct; La Granja(10 km).

Doctor Velasco 9, 40003, Segovia
Tel (911) 431201
Location on steep hill inside city walls; signed from the aqueduct; with private car parking
Meals breakfast, bar snacks
Prices rooms 6,800-11,000pts; breakfast 600pts
Rooms 40 double, 5 single, 10 suites, all with bath; all rooms have central heating, phone, radio; most rooms have TV
Facilities bar/breakfast area, sitting-room, conference room, terrace
Credit cards AE, DC, MC ,V
Children welcome
Disabled lift/elevator to all rooms
Pets not accepted
Closed never
Manager Miguel Borreguero

Paradores in Central Spain

The three provinces to the north-west of Madrid have a handful of interesting Paradores. The 73-room one at Tordesillas is a low modern building set in a secluded pine-grove, just out of the town; it makes a good base for exploring this very interesting region of castles and medieval towns (Tel (983) 770051). Within easy reach of it is the PN de Segovia – modern, 80 rooms, on the edge of a lake, fine views of the town and cathedral (Tel (911) 430462). Near Avila is the 15thC PN Raimundo de Borgoña (see page 109) and, in the Sierra de Gredos, the rustic PN de Gredos near Navarredonda de Gredos, with its beamed ceilings and mounted hunting trophies (Tel (918) 348048).

With one exception, the Paradores to the north-east of Madrid (Soria and Sigüenza) and to the south (Chinchon, Toledo, Almagro, Alarcón) are all described in detail in this section. The exception is the unremarkable PN de Manzanares, east of Ciudad Real, which is a large white modern building in shady grounds (Tel (926) 613600).

Segovia

Village hotel, Pedraza de la Sierra

La Posada de Don Mariano

If you are lucky, and it is a quiet night, Jesús Luis Gómez, the manager of this archetypal charming small hotel, will offer you a selection of rooms. The trouble is: which one do you choose if all of them are like showpieces from an antiquated Ideal Home Exhibition?

Each is unique, personal, luxuriously carpeted and decorated with English floral wallpaper. Antiques abound. Everything is carefully arranged and prepared so that you could almost forget you are in a hotel. It comes as no surprise to learn that the hotel was designed by the owner of one of Madrid's most famous furnishing shops and was recently featured in *Elle* magazine. But that does not help you choose your room. Maybe you should just take your chance. How about one of the attic rooms upstairs? Smaller perhaps, but still exquisitely furnished and oozing with character.

We had three minor reservations about the hotel: the noise from the bar below seems to travel to the rooms above it; the bathrooms are inadequately lit; and breakfast is disappointing. Otherwise, this is a hotel to remember.

Nearby Castle and square (2 mins walk each); scenic road up to Puerto de Navafría in the Sierra de Guadarrama (30 km).

Calle Mayor 14, 40172,
Pedraza de la Sierra, Segovia
Tel (911) 509886
Location near castle in main street; no private car parking
Meals breakfast
Prices rooms 8,000-10,000pts; breakfast 500-800pts
Rooms 15 double, 3 single, all with bath; all rooms have central heating, phone, TV
Facilities breakfast room/bar
Credit cards AE, DC, MC, V

Children welcome
Disabled access impossible
Pets not accepted
Closed never
Manager Mariano Pascual

Soria

Modern Parador, Soria

PN Antonio Machado

Prettily located, hanging off the side of a very green hilltop park, this modern brick-built Parador could be seen as a short guide to modern Spanish literature. It is named after the poet who lived and wrote in Soria but died in exile; you will find his blown-up image and his more famous poems on many of the pinkish walls.

Unlike most other modern Paradors, this one has not been contrived to look old. The furniture is as recent as the building and is occasionally brash and uncomfortable – but it may come as something of a relief after the rustic Castilian style of so many other Paradors. And if the hotel is short on charm, it has the compensating virtue of small size.

The entrance and reception are half-way up the building. There are bedrooms on the two floors above it and on one below. The higher up you go, of course, the better the view: 12 of the higher rooms offer vistas of Soria and the surrounding woodland; the rest are too low to see much from, or else look directly on to the quiet one-way road around the park outside. The dining- room and sitting-room are open-plan, separated by a wooden screen and sharing the same high, sloping ceiling; noise, unfortunately, travels easily between them.

Nearby: San Juan de Duero monastery (1.5 km).

parque del Castillo, 42005, Soria
Tel (975) 213445
Location on hill overlooking city and Duero river; with car parking
Meals breakfast, lunch, dinner
Prices rooms 9,500-11,000pts; breakfast 1,100pts, dinner 3,200pts
Rooms 28 double, 4 single, 2 suites, all with bath; all rooms have central heating,

air-conditioning, phone, TV, minibar
Facilities dining-room, 2 sitting-rooms, bar
Credit cards AE, DC, MC, V
Children welcome
Disabled access impossible
Pets not accepted
Closed never
Manager Emilio Lafuente

Ávila

City hotel, Ávila

Gran Hotel Palacio Valderrábanos

From its grand 15thC stone doorway, surmounted by an aristo-cratic family crest, to a room with a private tower, this spacious and calm hotel is pervaded by its past. Over reception you will find a graceful stone arch and old painted beams. In the hall, a glass case crammed full of antiques and curios for sale makes souvenir hunting easy.

The older, cosier rooms have floral wallpaper and beech furni-ture, but they occasionally feel uncomfortably half-empty. The thick shutters – which cut out noise – also shut out the daylight (the modern rooms on the third floor are much lighter). Some of the rooms have views across the square to the magnificent door of Ávila cathedral. But the real treat among them is room 229, from which a staircase ascends to a secluded sitting-room in the former watch-tower.

The slightly rustic white-walled restaurant in the basement (more attractive than the marbled dining-room upstairs) could be a museum of cookery – its intriguing exhibits including gigantic wine pots, an old sausage press (medieval, we were assured) and a vintage cheese churn.

Nearby Cathedral (opposite hotel), city walls (5 mins walk), St Thomas' Monastery (short drive); Guisando stone bulls (70 km).

plaza Catedral 9, 05001, Ávila
Tel (918) 211023
Location next to cathedral in middle of town; no private car parking
Meals breakfast, lunch, dinner
Prices rooms 7,200-19,300pts; breakfast 850pts, dinner 3,100pts
Rooms 62 double, 8 single, 3 suites, all with bath; all rooms have central heating, air-conditioning, phone, TV, minibar, radio, hairdrier
Facilities 2 dining-rooms, 3 sitting-rooms, bar
Credit cards AE, DC, MC, V
Children welcome
Disabled access easy; lift/elevator
Pets accepted
Closed never
Manager Tomas Beltran Ramirez

Ávila

City Parador, Ávila

PN Raimundo de Borgoña

In a corner of the old town, nestling against the city walls, this Parador is a careful mixture of old and new. Only the distinctive tower, and the shady courtyard with its tall pine tree, are left of the original building.

The rooms, like the building, divide into the old and the new. Those in the tower are somewhat cramped, with squeaky wooden floors. Those in the modern wings are larger, lighter and have better views. Some have four-poster beds. In others, the bed-frames look as if they had been made from sawn-up portcullises. In spring, birdwatchers should ask for room 209, from which there is a good view of storks nesting on an old belltower between March and June.

There are not many inviting places to sit indoors, but there is a sunny terrace outside the bar, and the courtyard is always fresh and cool. From the pleasant grounds at the front of the hotel you can climb up on to Ávila's famous city walls.

The restaurant serves a special dessert: soft, sweet balls named after Ávila's famous daughter – 'Saint Teresa's Yolks'.

Nearby Polentinos Palace and cathedral (5 mins walk); St Thomas' Monastery (a short drive); Guisando stone bulls (70 km); Sierra de Gredos (80 km).

Marqués de Canales y Chozas 16, 05001, Ávila
Tel (918) 211340
Location near old walls in middle of city; small car park
Meals breakfast, lunch, dinner
Prices rooms 8,500-11,000pts; breakfast 1,100pts, dinner 3,200pts
Rooms 59 double, 3 single, all with bath; all rooms have central heating, phone, TV, minibar, hairdrier

Facilities dining-room, sitting-room, bar, patio
Credit cards AE, DC, MC, V
Children welcome
Disabled access difficult; lift/elevator to 5 rooms
Pets not accepted
Closed never
Manager Juan de la Torre Alcala

Madrid

Hotels in Madrid

Hotels in the city of Madrid cannot be conveniently divided into districts; they spread throughout the central area. The heart of the city is bounded by the Palacio Real and the railway terminus of the Estación del Norte on the west, and the wonderful Prado museum and gardens of El Retiro on the east, with the plaza of the Puerta del Sol roughly in the middle.

The Arosa (Tel (91) 532 1600) is a stylish building on the Gran Via, close to the Puerta del Sol. The rooms are elaborately decorated and well soundproofed to minimise noise from the busy street below. Also close to the Puerta del Sol is the Victoria (Tel (91) 531 4500), an old favourite, with 120 reasonably priced rooms. The best of these overlook the pretty little plaza of Santa Ana.

Madrid is not blessed with the little gem-like hotels that are such a feature of Paris, Venice or Florence, for example. Real quality tends to go hand in hand with size and grandeur (and expense). For a once-in-a-blue-moon treat, there is the Ritz (Tel (91) 521 2857), which has been beautifully restored to reflect its former early-19thC glory. Public rooms are decorated with priceless carpets and tapestries, bedrooms are filled with antiques, service is absolutely immaculate; this is one of Spain's top hotels, a fact reflected in its prices. Nearby is the equally grand but rather less wonderful Palace (Tel (91) 429 7551), a massive 500-room hotel with an impressive clientele – from matadors to politicians. Service tends to be (not surprisingly) rather impersonal, but like the Ritz it has an excellent location close to the Prado. In contrast, the Villa Magna (Tel (91) 561 4900) is further from the middle towards the northern district. It is a modern version of the Ritz, and almost as classy. Set in immaculate gardens, it has a glass and steel tower, public rooms decorated in 18thC style, large bedrooms and stylish dining-rooms.

Outside the central area, there are two hotels worth mentioning. The Monte Real (Tel (91) 216 2140) is a modern hotel in an exclusive suburb. Ask for one of the rooms that overlooks the pool surrounded by trees in tranquil gardens. The hotel is far more impressive from the inside than from the outside; walls are hung with fabulous works of art and tapestries. The Barajas (Tel (91) 747 7700) is 14 km from the middle of the city, near the airport – ideal for anyone with an early flight. It has excellent facilities, including a swimming-pool, gymnasium, golf course and gardens.

Paying by credit card
We say in our factboxes which credit cards are accepted. Whether you do or do not value the free credit gained when paying by card, there are other advantages, particularly when making a payment in advance. Provided the card is a genuine credit card which permits you to borrow money for an extended period (Visa, Mastercard) and not a charge card which lacks that facility (American Express, Diners Club), paying with the card makes the credit card company jointly liable for fulfilment of your contract with the hotel. If you are not given the kind of room you wanted, for example, you can pursue a claim against the credit company when you get home.

Madrid

City hotel, Madrid

Hotel Carlos V

A busily popular hotel in a pedestrianized street next to the Puerta del Sol ('the centre of Spain'), the Carlos V may be infuriating to find in a car, but it could not be nearer the heart of the Spanish capital.

There has been much modernization lately, some of it thoughtless. Nevertheless, there are a few remaining handsome red-wood door frames in the public areas, and remnants of stained glass (not to mention the statutory suit of armour in the entrance hall). And the sitting-room remains an exceptionally stylish and elegant place, with comfortable sofas – some of them made of bamboo – crystal chandeliers, large mirrors, and a moulded ceiling.

The bedrooms are impersonal but they have bright modern bathrooms. Some rooms on the first and second floors have small balconies, and five rooms at the top of the building have fair-sized, sun-catching terraces which are worth asking for.

A central location, however, has its disadvantages. A good night's sleep in the Carlos V in summer depends on getting the right balance between ventilation, street noise and the din of the air-conditioning.

Nearby Metro (Callao or Sol, 2 mins walk), Plaza Mayor.

Maestro Vitoria 5, 28013, Madrid
Tel (91) 531 4100
Location on a pedestrianized street near Puerta del Sol; public car parking nearby
Meals breakfast
Prices rooms 11,250pts; breakfast 600pts
Rooms 61 double, 6 single, all with bath; all rooms have central heating, air-conditioning, phone, TV, radio
Facilities sitting-room, bar/breakfast room
Credit cards AE, DC, MC, V
Children welcome
Disabled access easy; lift/elevator
Pets not accepted
Closed never
Proprietor Nicolas Gutierrez Herrera

Madrid

City hotel, Madrid

Hotel Serrano

On a side street off Madrid's prestigious, modern north-south axis, the Paseo de la Castellana (the place to be seen these days), the Serrano is a small hotel for anyone in search of a little non-central exclusivity.

The building – unashamedly modern, with a grimy façade – is well designed inside, with plenty of light and space. Moreover, it has been conscientiously decorated and furnished, often with reproduction period chairs and tables. There are also a few genuinely antique objects. The large, sombre 18thC tapestry on the wall of the sitting-room-cum-bar is, we were assured, a price-less national treasure.

In a Spanish city hotel with so few rooms, you can expect some extras – such as special massage showers in all bathrooms. The three suites are moderately luxurious; their sitting-rooms alone are bigger than many entire hotel rooms. There are even maga-zines on the coffee tables – a personal touch for a chain hotel.

Warts and all, here you get the feeling that you are one of a very few select guests and can make yourself a little at home. A modest alternative to the Ritz at a fraction of the price.

Nearby Metro (Rubén Darío station, 5 mins walk); the Prado and Retiro Park (2 km); Plaza Mayor and old city centre (3 km).

Marqués de Villamejor 8, 28006, Madrid
Tel (91) 435 5200
Location in a quiet street near Paseo de la Castellana; no private car parking
Meals breakfast
Prices rooms 8,500-19,000pts; breakfast 850pts
Rooms 28 double, 3 single, 3 suites, all with bath; all rooms have central heating, air-conditioning, phone, TV, minibar, hairdrier
Facilities sitting-room/bar
Credit cards AE, DC, MC, V
Children welcome
Disabled access difficult; lift/elevator
Pets not accepted
Closed never
Manager Benito Anselmo Gil

Madrid

Converted monastery, Chinchón

PN de Chinchón

Gathered around a light, green, airy courtyard – with tall cypress trees in its corners and pigeons flitting around a fountain and climbing roses – the ground floor of this 17thC monastery is a wealth of colour and detail. The peaceful, glazed-in cloisters form wide passages which are decorated with murals and antiques: clocks, chests, cabinets, even a large old brass still (the town is renowned for its *anis*).

The stately dining-room and cool blue bar are both brightly tiled and lit by small windows piercing massively thick walls. Climb the staircase, which has original but fading frescoes on the ceiling above it, and you find landings furnished with comfortable sofas.

The bedrooms are different in style from everything else. They have the austere but romantic atmosphere of a decaying medieval palace: very clean, but deliberately made to look as if they were a little dusty; with the shutters closed tightly, little daylight penetrates the gloom. The floors are covered with earth-red tiles and the blue wooden furniture is brightly painted with golden garlands – quite out of character with the nobility of the ground floor. They have generously-sized Parador bathrooms.

Nearby Plaza Mayor; Royal Palace, Aranjuez (26 km).

avenida Generalisimo 1, 28370, Chinchón, Madrid
Tel (91) 894 0836
Location opposite main square in heart of village; private garage
Meals breakfast, lunch, dinner
Prices rooms 12,500-14,000pts; breakfast 1,200pts, dinner 3,500pts
Rooms 38 double, all with bath; all rooms have central heating, air-conditioning, phone, TV, minibar, hairdrier
Facilities 2 dining-rooms, sitting-room, bar, terrace
Credit cards AE ,DC ,MC, V
Children welcome
Disabled access not easy; some ground-floor rooms
Pets not accepted
Closed never
Manager Antonio Bertolin Blasco

Madrid

Converted cloister, El Paular

Hotel Santa María de El Paular

You don't often get the chance to stay in a four-star hotel next to – and sharing its premises with – a Benedictine monastery. The Santa María occupies the old cloisters, entered by means of a monumental arch.

Sadly, the chain that runs this hotel is more interested in its up-market facility-rich image than in artistic heritage. The mock-historical style of decoration scarcely does justice to the hand-some surroundings. You will just have to use your imagination. But it is a peaceful place, surrounded by trees and with plenty of space to stretch out – a popular location for conferences and wedding receptions. There is also a choice of places to eat. Apart from the dining-room, a *méson* offers lamb cooked in the tradit-ional way, in a wood-fired oven.

The bedrooms are simple, sober and Castilian in style – which in this part of the world tends to mean that they have charac-terless woodwork and wrought iron light fittings. You might prefer to call them austere or spartan: more suitable for a monastic retreat, and certainly less than you would expect from this class of hotel. Most have views of either the courtyard or the garden, and the grand mountains beyond.

Nearby Monastery church (next door).

28741, El Paular, Madrid
Tel (91) 869 1011
Location in mountains of Sierra de Guadarrama, near village; with garden and car parking
Meals breakfast, lunch, dinner
Prices rooms 7,500-22,000pts; breakfast 1,550pts, dinner 4,275pts
Rooms 36 double, all with bath; 17 single, 2 with bath, 15 with shower; 5 suites, all with bath; all rooms have central heating, phone, TV
Facilities 2 dining-rooms, sitting-room, bar, games room; swimming-pool, tennis courts, mountain bikes
Credit cards AE, DC, MC, V
Children welcome; special play area
Disabled access difficult
Pets not accepted
Closed never **Manager** Enrique Gonzalez Otero

Guadalajara

Castle Parador, Sigüenza

PN Castillo de Sigüenza

Other castles seem small in comparison with this massive example, which stands defiantly alone on a hill above the town that it guards, at the top of a steep cobbled street.

Unfortunately, the most interesting bits – the towers and battlements – are out of bounds. But there is plenty left to explore. Near Room 239, for example, an inconspicuous slit in the wall leads to a secret balcony high over the silent chapel.

The sitting-room ('the throne room'), held up by six stone pillars and containing two fireplaces, is big enough for giants to repose in, and is sprinkled with regal chairs crowned with gold knobs. The layout is rather formal, in contrast to the inviting stone-arched bar, with its benches and leather chairs.

The bedrooms come with or without overhanging wooden balconies overlooking the large courtyard, with its ornamental hedges and soothingly gurgling fountain, but one balcony (Room 210) dangles daringly over the castle's outer walls. Seven rooms have four-poster beds, but they are not reservable by phone. The walls between rooms are not all of fortress proportions; we found that the noise of other guests' televisions, plumbing and conversations travelled easily.

Nearby Roman arch at Medinacelli (20 km), Atienza (30 km).

plaza del Castillo, 19250, Sigüenza, Guadalajara
Tel (911) 390100
Location on hill overlooking town, at top of steep cobbled street; with car park
Meals breakfast, lunch, dinner
Prices rooms 8,500-10,500pts; breakfast 900pts, dinner 2,700pts
Rooms 74 double, 2 single, all with bath; all rooms have central heating,
air-conditioning, phone, TV, minibar
Facilities dining-room, sitting-room, bar, patio
Credit cards AE, DC, MC, V
Children welcome
Disabled access easy; lift/elevator
Pets not accepted
Closed never
Manager Juan Carlos Sanchez Galvez

Toledo

Country house hotel, Toledo

La Almazara

Just a few kilometres out of Toledo is this lovely hotel on a wooded hilltop overlooking the city. The views are magnificent – and cost half the price of the Parador further around the hill. It is a simple, rustic place, built as a country residence in the 16thC. A gravel courtyard is surrounded on three sides by a solid ivy-clad building; the hotel rooms are on two of these sides, while the owner's home forms the third.

This is not the sort of place you would want to lounge around in all day, and it does not have a restaurant, but it is the perfect haven after a hot day's sightseeing in touristy Toledo. The staff are friendly and the atmosphere is very laid back. The huge sitting-room looks just like home – comfy sofas around a log fire, piles of magazines and books scattered on tables, and a TV in one corner. Breakfast is served in a delightful arched room that leads on to a small (and rather overgrown) terrace. All the bedrooms are simple, cool and spacious (extra beds can be installed), and are brightened up by locally-made curtains and bedspreads. Bedrooms 1 to 9 all have balconies overlooking Toledo.

Nearby Toledo – Alcázar, cathedral, El Greco museum, synagogue and Jewish quarter; Madrid (70 km).

Apartado Postal 6, 48080, Toledo
Tel (925) 223866
Location on hill overlooking Toledo; 3 km from Carretera Circunvalación, on Cuerva road; with car parking in courtyard
Meals breakfast
Prices rooms 3,000-5,500pts; breakfast 400pts
Rooms 19 double, 2 single, all with bath; all rooms have central heating, phone
Facilities sitting-room, breakfast room
Credit cards AE, DC, MC, V
Children welcome
Disabled 6 ground-floor rooms
Pets not accepted
Closed Nov to mid-Mar
Proprietor Juan Manuel Cavero-Carondelet

Toledo

Town mansion, Toledo

Hostal del Cardenal

This classy little hotel was one of the highlights of our 1990 inspection tour. It occupies a long, pale-brick mansion, built in the 18thC as the summer residence of the archbishop of Toledo, Cardinal Lorenzana. It is set in beautiful shaded gardens, virtually enclosed by the old city walls, rising in three tiers to an impressive, crested doorway. The lowest tier of the garden incorporates an excellent restaurant, now run independently but used by all the guests.

Every room oozes style and character; the sitting-rooms contain well-chosen antiques, the stairway has a beautiful sculpted ceiling, bedrooms have old painted-wood bedheads, and bathrooms have hand-painted tiles and old mirrors. There is a clever mixture of old and new throughout; original Moorish corbels support beams in the upstairs corridor, while modern Moorish sculpture surrounds bedroom doors downstairs. There are two brick courtyards, decorated with ferns, terracotta pots and lilies.

This is a magical place to enjoy a warm summer's evening. You need to book well in advance as it is extremely popular, especially with British and American tourists.

Nearby Alcázar, cathedral, El Greco Museum, synagogue and Jewish quarter; Madrid (70 km).

Paseo de Recaredo 24, 45004, Toledo
Tel (925) 224900
Location within city walls near main gate (Puerta de Bisagra); with garden but no private car parking
Meals breakfast; lunch and dinner in adjacent restaurant of same name
Prices rooms 5,300-12,800pts; breakfast 550pts, dinner in restaurant 2,500pts

Rooms 22 double, 2 suites, all with bath; all rooms have central heating, phone; most have air-conditioning, hairdrier, TV, minibar
Facilities breakfast room, 2 sitting-rooms
Credit cards AE, DC, MC, V
Children welcome
Disabled no special facilities
Pets accepted
Closed never
Proprietor José Gonzalez

Toledo

Hilltop Parador, Toledo

PN Conde de Orgaz

Situated on a hillside just south of the city, this Parador is understandably on practically every coach party itinerary; some stay, some dine and some simply come to admire the view of Toledo – it is a magical place from which to watch the sun setting over the sandy domes and spires. Most bedrooms share the view, at least to some degree. All the rooms we saw were large and comfortable, with brightly coloured rugs on red stone floors, and blue and white tiled bathrooms.

The Parador is entirely modern, built in the same sandy stone as the city and perched right on the edge of a cliff, among rocks and shrubby vegetation. Despite the hotel's youth, the public rooms have a traditional flavour – ceilings are beamed, walls are decorated with copper pans, pottery plates, and ceramic tiles. The sitting-room has a huge open fireplace surrounded by stone wall seats. There is a smaller lounge (with bar and cafeteria), opening on to a terrace which runs the length of the front of the hotel. The two dining-rooms serve expensive meals (even by Parador standards) but most people would agree that it is well worth paying for the superb view.

Nearby Toledo – Alcazar, cathedral, El Greco museum, synagogue and Jewish quarter; Madrid (70 km).

Paseo de los Cigarrales, 45000, Toledo
Tel (925) 221850
Location on hill south of Toledo overlooking city; with garden and car parking
Meals breakfast, lunch, dinner
Prices rooms 13,000-14,000pts; breakfast 1,200pts; meals 3,500pts
Rooms 71 double, 6 single, all with bath; all rooms have central heating,
air-conditioning, phone, TV, minibar, hairdrier
Facilities 2 dining-rooms, sitting-room, bar, TV room; swimming-pool
Credit cards AE, DC, MC, V
Children welcome
Disabled access difficult
Pets not accepted
Closed never
Manager Fernando Molina Aranda

Cuenca

Country hotel, Cuenca

Hotel La Cueva del Fraile

Set in the same green, high-walled valley as the city of Cuenca, this is a larger hotel than at first it appears to be, and the 16thC ancestry to which it lays claim is scarcely in evidence, for all its blackened beams. But the hotel, gathered around a brilliant-white courtyard, does have many other virtues.

There is a great variety of public rooms on the ground floor taking in numerous seating areas and a rather gloomy bar with comfortable settees. There is also a good choice of activities, including a pool and tennis court, and bicycles for hire. The hotel has a children's play area. The bedrooms are divided into the old, the new and the very new. In almost all of them the 'old' wooden beams of the ceiling clash with the new white wood of the doors and cupboards. If you want something special, room 130 is a tasteful suite with a cottage-style sitting room and rocking chairs.

The hotel makes an excellent base for excursions to Cuenca and its scenic surroundings. Ask Fernando on reception for the best places to go: he is the co-author of one of the best guide books to the area.

Nearby Cuenca; Ventano del Diablo (30 km); Ciudad Encantada (45 km).

Carretera de Buenache, Hoz del río Húecar, 16001, Cuenca **Tel** (966) 211571
Location in gorge of river Húecar, 7 km from Cuenca on Buenache road; with garden and car parking
Meals breakfast, lunch, dinner
Prices B&B 5,500-9,500pts; breakfast 575pts; dinner 2,300pts
Rooms 52 double, 9 single, 2 family rooms, all with bath; all have central heating, phone
Facilities 3 dining-rooms, 5 sitting-rooms, bar, billiards room, dance floor; swimming-pool, tennis court
Credit cards AE, DC, MC, V
Children welcome; special play area; baby-sitting available
Disabled access easy; 8 ground-floor rooms **Pets** not accepted **Closed** Jan and Feb
Proprietor Borja Garcia Herrero

Cuenca

Town house hotel, Cuenca

Posada de San José

Once the home of the in-laws of Velazquez's daughter and later a cathedral choir school, this Posada could hardly offer better credentials. Today – with a 1961 addition – it is a six-tier labyrinth replete with curios, antique furniture and even frescos. If you like stairs, antiques, history and exploring, this is the hotel for you.

Jennifer Morter, an expatriate Canadian, and her Spanish husband Antonio have lovingly decorated every room with great attention to detail and cleanliness ('you could sit on the floor', Jennifer likes to say). The sheets are pressed and turned back in the old-fashioned way. The 25 rooms are all different and each has been given individual character – you may get a four-poster bed, a Latin inscription on the wall or a dreamy balcony with a magnificent view across the valley. Room 33 is the most popular, with its sloping floor and two balconies.

The rooms themselves are cosy enough to sit in but there is also a rambling breakfast room/bar with intimate nooks and a sunny terrace, a TV room stranded on its own peculiar floor and a hall with a few antiques and a sofa.

Nearby Cathedral and Casas Colgadas (both within a short walk); Ventano del Diablo (25 km), Ciudad Encantada (35 km).

Calle Julian Romero 4, 16000, Cuenca
Tel (966) 211300
Location off Plaza Mayor in old part of town, down narrow road past cathedral; no private car parking
Meals breakfast
Prices rooms 3,000-6,250pts; breakfast 375pts
Rooms 12 double, 7 with bath; 5 single, 2 with shower; 8 family rooms, 7 with bath; all rooms have central heating
Facilities breakfast room, TV room, bar
Credit cards AE
Children welcome
Disabled access impossible
Pets accepted
Closed never
Proprietor Jennifer Morter and Antonio Cortinas Vega

Cuenca

Castle Parador, Alarcón

PN Marqués de Villena

You may not believe your eyes as you approach Alarcón, so improbable is the position of the castle which has guarded the village since Moorish times – overlooking the valley of the deep-green Río Júcar, on the edge of Don Quixote's La Mancha.

You may feel like a wandering knight returning from the Crusades as you step into the quaint little courtyard with its well in the middle. Within the thick castle walls you should sleep well and live in typical Parador style, with your minibar discreetly hidden in a reproduction antique cabinet; the pick of the bedrooms is number 103, with a canopied bed and steps up to a high window where distressed damsels might sit and dream of rescue. The sitting-room-cum-cafeteria has everything you could want of a great hall: a circular iron chandelier, an enormous tapestry depicting a coat of arms, a suit of armour and three wooden thrones. The dining room is also a vaulted chamber, with a long slit window.

A lift will whisk you up to the battlements for a view worthy of a feudal baron. The village has several other historical buildings and there are some good walks.

Nearby Castle of Belmonte (70 km), Mota del Cuervo (85 km) and Cuenca (85 km).

Avenida Amigos del Castillo, 16213, Alarcón, Cuenca
Tel (966) 331350
Location on huge rock encircled by river, at end of village; car parking outside castle
Meals breakfast, lunch, dinner
Prices rooms 12,000-13,500pts; breakfast 1,100pts, dinner 3,200pts
Rooms 12 double, one single, all with bath; all rooms have central heating, phone, TV, minibar
Facilities dining-room, sitting-room, bar
Credit cards AE, DC, MC, V
Children welcome; special play area
Disabled access difficult; lift/elevator
Pets not accepted
Closed never
Manager José Menguiano Corbacho

Cuenca

Town hotel, Mota del Cuervo

Mesón de Don Quijote

If Don Quixote himself was not to be taken too seriously, then neither is his *mesón*, which is inauspiciously located behind a petrol station in a little town overlooked by windmills in the heart of La Mancha.

The whole ground floor – with its cartwheel chandeliers, theatrical staircase, papier-maché well and cobbled inn-court-yard-cum-lounge (where the ingenious hidalgo could easily have been knighted) – flirts with the memory of Cervantes' hero. All that is lacking is the buxom Dulcinea. Fixtures and fittings are typically 'rustic' and Castilian – history as it never was. The chunky dining- room chairs, all nuts and bolts, must have been a fascinating woodwork project for somebody. The bar-stools are reminiscent of something out of a medieval torture chamber.

The waiters are dressed in 'traditional' costume, with broad red cummerbunds, grey waistcoats and bootlace ties. The restaurant's excellent menu includes a hearty vegetarian bean soup and home-made rice pudding.

Unfortunately, the rustic illusion stops short of the bedrooms, which are fairly nondescript. But the rest of the hotel should keep you well entertained.

Nearby Belmonte Castle (15 km); El Toboso (15 km).

Francisco Costi 2, 16630, Mota del Cuervo, Cuenca
Tel (967) 180200
Location behind filling station on main road through town; with car parking
Meals breakfast, lunch, dinner
Prices rooms 4,547-8,926pts; breakfast 475pts,
Rooms 28 double, 7 single, one suite, all with bath; all rooms have central heating, air-conditioning, phone

Facilities dining-room, 3 sitting-rooms, bar; swimming-pool
Credit cards AE, DC, MC, V
Children accepted
Disabled access difficult
Pets not accepted
Closed never
Proprietor José Maria Palacios Maso

Ciudad Real

Converted convent Parador, Almagro

PN de Almagro

Almagro's Parador has ancient origins (it is on the site of a 16thC Franciscan convent) but is almost entirely modern, built just a decade ago. The layout of the building is highly unusual – the rooms are set around sixteen little quads, all different from each other. The first one you come to has ivy-clad walls and fig trees shading a small fountain, the second bamboo trees around a pond, the third rose-bushes, and so on.

It would be easy to get lost inside – every corridor looks the same – if it were not for the lovely hand-painted signs and room numbers on every corner. Such attention to detail runs throughout – there are painted ceilings and bright tapestries in the public rooms, tiled bed-heads and locally made lace covers in the bedrooms, and fresh flowers throughout. The *bodega* is built on two floors in the old cellars of the convent; massive storage jars go up through the floor and are used as table tops on the upper level. Other cosy sitting-rooms are dotted about.

Despite its size, this is one of the friendliest Paradors – an interesting place in a picturesque town on the plains of Don Quixote's La Mancha.

Nearby Plaza Mayor, old town, lace-making; Ciudad Real (25 km); Valdepeñas (35 km).

Ronda de San Francisco, 13270, Almagro, Ciudad Real
Tel (926) 860100
Location in quiet street, near centre of town, signed from main road; with garden and car parking
Meals breakfast, lunch, dinner
Prices rooms 9,000-11,000pts; breakfast 1,100pts; dinner 3,200pts
Rooms 48 double, 6 single, one family room; all with bath; all rooms have central heating, air-conditioning, phone, TV, minibar
Facilities 2 dining-rooms, 2 sitting-rooms, bar, terrace; swimming-pool
Credit cards AE, DC, MC, V
Children welcome
Disabled access easy
Pets not accepted
Closed never
Manager José Munoz Romera

Teruel

Converted palace, Albarracín

Hotel Albarracín

Near the top of a steep, cobbled street leading to Aragon's unspoiled, rose-tinted medieval village stands the fine 16thC Gothic palace which is now the Hotel Albarracín. Stepping inside the hall is no disappointment – like stepping back in time, so atmospheric is the stately old building, with its black wooden beams, stag's head on the wall and subdued lighting.

The illusion is not maintained for long. The present management has not realized the palace's potential, and the furnishings, which pretend to give a sense of history, fall far short of the real thing. The public rooms are characterized by their wrought iron light fittings, dark wood and bunches of plastic flowers. But the sitting-room has some more sincere touches including a large green ceramic mural in the typical style of Teruel. Impressive views across the valley can be seen from many of the windows, and some of the bedrooms. The bathrooms are unfortunately decorated in a garish colour scheme.

The hotel is quiet and has a swimming pool at the bottom of the stepped garden. Best of all, it is well located for exploring the narrow streets of the splendid old town, which has deservedly been declared a National Monument.

Nearby Teruel (40 km), Montes Universales (10 km).

Calle Azagra, 44100, Albarracín, Teruel
Tel (974) 710011
Location in small square, close to old village centre; no private car parking
Meals breakfast, lunch, dinner
Prices rooms 9,975; breakfast 600pts, dinner 2,580pts
Rooms 38 double, 2 single, all with bath; all rooms have central heating, phone, TV (satellite)

Facilities dining-room, TV room, bar; swimming-pool
Credit cards AE, DC, MC, V
Children welcome
Disabled access possible
Pets accepted in bedrooms
Closed never
Proprietor Francisco José Marcelino

Teruel

Historic village inn, Mirambel

Fonda Guimerá

Take a walled medieval village – complete with watch- tower, numerous Gothic palaces and wide cobbled streets – restore all these elements carefully, and what you have is Mirambel, once acclaimed the 'most beautiful village in Spain' by Queen Sofía.

The old *fonda* has also been restored. Its façade on the main street is in keeping with the rest of this historic village but everything behind it is ultra-new. All the bedrooms are modern and comfortable. Although half provide nothing more than basic accommodation, those at the back of the building have small bathrooms and balconies, and the central heating is needed in winter.

The Fonda is a simple, inexpensive place to stay and it does not have a sitting-room or any other public facilities. But you can always have a drink with the locals in the small, gloomy public bar next door which doubles as reception (don't be put off by its appearance), and with a restaurant behind.

The village itself is a fascinating place to stroll around and is set in magnificent countryside, reminiscent of the Yorkshire Dales, which is good for walking and cycling. It is still just off the beaten tourist track, and worth the detour.

Nearby Cantavieja (15 km), Morella (30 km).

Calle Agustín Pastor 28,
44000, Mirambel, Teruel
Tel (964) 185011
Location on cobbled street in village; no private car parking
Meals breakfast, lunch, dinner
Prices rooms 1,400-1,800pts; menu 750pts
Rooms 10 double, 5 with bath; all rooms have 5 rooms have central heating
Facilities dining-room, bar
Credit cards not accepted

Children welcome
Disabled access difficult
Pets not accepted
Closed never
Manager Pedro Guimerá

Teruel

Castle Parador, Alcañiz

PN La Concordia

Still dominating the town and its green river from the summit of a hill, as it has done since the 12th century, this castle-monastery is the first thing that you see as you approach Alcañiz; it certainly looks too big to have only 12 rooms.

Although monumental in scale, the former home of the Order of the Knights of Calatrava has been converted into an intimate hotel full of historical character. It is furnished in a modern imitation of castle-style, with wrought iron chandeliers everywhere and gold knobs topping the chairs in a dining-room fit for medieval banquets. In the bedrooms, however, you can forget that you are in a castle, as evidence of the past has been largely crowded out by new furnishings. There are magnificent views from most of the rooms and the rest look on to the peaceful cloister-garden behind.

The castle is also a tourist attraction and its grounds are open to the public – so it is not a place in which to seek seclusion. The TV in the cafeteria at the entrance, in an elegant vaulted chamber, sometimes intrudes too, but at night the castle returns more or less to its ancestral peace.

Nearby Caspe (30 km) – Roman temple, caves of Molinos (40 km), El Parrisal near Beceite (50 km) – wildlife.

Castillo de los Calatravos, 44600, Alcañiz, Teruel
Tel (974) 830400
Location on hill dominating town (follow Parador signs); with garden and car parking
Meals breakfast, lunch, dinner
Prices rooms 9,000-11,500pts; breakfast 1,100pts, dinner 3,200pts
Rooms 10 double, 2 single, all with bath; all rooms have central heating,
air-conditioning, phone, TV, minibar
Facilities 2 dining-rooms, 2 sitting-rooms, cafeteria
Credit cards AE, DC, MC, V
Children welcome
Disabled access easy; lift/elevator
Pets not accepted
Closed early Dec to Jan
Manager Miguel Cruz Sanchez

Castellón

Converted palace, Morella

Hotel Cardenal Ram

Cardinal Ram's 16thC Gothic palace, set in a commanding position on Morella's medieval porticoed main street, is a local landmark. Its thick walls enclose a variety of spacious rooms. The furnishings have seen better days and do not accord with the age and style of the building, and the beds tend to be too soft for comfort. But the bathrooms are modern and well-equipped, and the rooms on the 2nd and 3rd floors have magnificent views.

The excellent restaurant is well known for its local delicacies including the succulent *cordero trufado* – lamb stuffed with truffles – the hearty Morella soup and *tarta al whisky* – home-made ice-cream. (It is only fair to advise you that you can get the same fare at lower prices just down the road in another restaurant, Casa Roque, under the same management as Cardenal Ram.) The hotel breakfast, it must be said, is disappointingly ordinary even by Spanish standards.

The hotel lacks seating and recreational space, but it makes up for this with its age and character. It is arguably overpriced for the level of comfort offered, but you can eat well here and it is as close to the authentic history of Morella as you will get.

Nearby Castle and church; La Balma (25 km), Montalvana – cave paintings (25 km), Mirambel (30 km) – walled village.

Cuesta Suñer 1, 12300, Morella, Castellón
Tel (964) 160000
Location in heart of Morella, on main street; no private car parking
Meals breakfast, lunch, dinner
Prices rooms 4,500-6,000pts; breakfast 400pts, dinner 1,750pts
Rooms 18 double, 1 single, all with bath; all rooms have central heating, phone, TV

Facilities dining-room, hall/sitting-room
Credit cards AE, DC, MC, V
Children welcome
Disabled access difficult
Pets not accepted
Closed never
Proprietor Roque Gutierrez Romero

Castellón

Town house hotel, Morella

Hostal Elías

Centrally located within the walls of the magnificent medieval hill-top town of Morella, Hostal Elías occupies a tastefully modernised town house, sparkling clean and excellent value.

All the rooms vary slightly but most of them are large. Some have small entrance halls separating the bathroom from the bedroom; others small sitting-rooms; and most of them have thin balconies looking over a picturesque street and catching the morning or evening sun. The wooden furniture is simple, and of varying antiquity and attractiveness – but always adequate, with plenty of storage. Rooms at the top of the building, although smaller, are cosy and have great views.

Señor Elías is quiet but a very friendly man and a mine of information to be plundered when the tourist office is closed (which it seems to be for much of the year).

Although Hostal Elías does not serve food, a short walk brings you to Morella's main street, which has several bars and restaurants, including the excellent Casa Roque – owned by the same people as the Cardenal Ram (page 127).

Nearby La Balma (25 km), Montalvana (35 km) – cave paintings, Mirambel (30 km) – walled village.

Calle Colomer 7, 12300, Morella, Castellón
Tel (964) 160092
Location in front of church on corner of two quiet streets; no private car parking
Meals not available
Prices rooms 1,500-4,500pts
Rooms 16 double, 1 single, all with bath; all rooms have central heating
Facilities sitting-room, TV room

Credit cards not accepted
Children welcome
Disabled access easy; 4 ground-floor rooms
Pets accepted
Closed 15 days in autumn
Proprietor Elias and Palmira Antoli Adell

Castellón

Hotel Aloha

Situated a little way back from the beach on the Costa del Azahar (the Orange Blossom Coast) the Aloha is a modern seaside hotel, with – let us be frank – no particular charm. But it is convenient and welcoming to return to after a day of sightseeing or sun-bathing, and it is clean, well-maintained and comfortable. The bedrooms have been recently redecorated and the furniture is emphatically modern – although softened by the widespread use of light wood. The better rooms look over the deep-blue swimming-pool towards the sea.

Nearby Castellón (20 km); Grottos of San José (20 km); Sagunto (35 km) – Roman Amphitheatre; Peñiscola (70 km).

Avenida Mediterraneo 75, 12530, Burriana, Castellón
Tel (964) 510104
Location on sea front, 200 m from beach; with garden and car parking
Meals breakfast, lunch, dinner
Prices rooms 4,800-5,600pts; breakfast 450pts, dinner 1,600pts
Rooms 27 double, 3 single, all with bath; all rooms have central heating, air-conditioning, phone, radio
Facilities dining-room, sitting-room, bar, terrace; swimming-pool
Credit cards V
Children welcome
Disabled lift/elevator
Pets not accepted
Closed never
Manager José Muñoe Romera

Hotel El Cid

With only the rather exclusive villa development of Las Playetas separating it from the sea, and set in its own palmy garden, decked with geraniums, the El Cid is well placed for a relaxing beach holiday. It is a modern block, uncompromising but functional – cool and bright, with tiled floors and furniture which can happily be flopped on while wearing a wet bikini. The bedrooms are well kept although rather bare, with the all-important shower or bath. The staff are a major asset, friendly and immediately helpful, and the four-course menus (changed every day) are good value.

Nearby beach; Benicasim (1.5 km); Castellón (9.5 km).

Las Playetas, 12594, Oropesa del Mar, Castellón
Tel (964) 300700
Location across road from beach; with car parking
Meals breakfast, lunch, dinner
Prices rooms 4,300-4,900pts; breakfast 400pts, lunch and dinner 1,400pts
Rooms 38 doubles, 34 with bath; 4 single with bath; 3 suites with bath; all rooms have phone
Facilities dining-room, sitting-room; swimming-pool, tennis court, minigolf
Credit cards MC, V
Children welcome; games room and play area
Disabled access easy; ground-floor rooms
Pets accepted in rooms
Closed Oct to Mar
Manager Odon Ofrego Llopis

Castellón

Seaside hotel, Peñíscola

Hostería del Mar

Though privately owned, this grand hostal with its own pool and garden is linked to the Paradors, and shares some of their characteristics. The welcome is friendly but formal, service satisfactory rather than solicitous.

Within sight of 15thC Peñíscola, the hotel has been given an interior which is self-consciously medieval, although the four-storey building itself is little more than 25 years old. The huge 'Golden Book' accompanying the suit of armour in reception, where guests can sign their names, has a leather cover that really is old. The old stove in the main salon is of similar vintage (yet still functions in winter).

The timbered dining-chambers accommodate 'period' banquets at regular intervals throughout the tourist season. But don't be put off: the normal dining-room is harmlessly rustic, and elsewhere there is plenty of opportunity for sinking into deep leather sofas.

The bedrooms have double-glazing, deckchairs on the balconies, hand-painted tiles in the bathrooms, and scatterings of Castilian furniture.

The beach is very handy – just across the road from the hotel.
Nearby Peñíscola (1.5 km); beach.

12598, Peñíscola, Castellón
Tel (964) 480600
Location set back from main promenade opposite sandy beach; with garden and garage
Meals breakfast, lunch, dinner
Prices rooms 9,200-12,500pts; breakfast 950pts, dinner 2,100pts
Rooms 64 double, 10 single, 11 family rooms, all with bath; all rooms have central heating, air-conditioning,

phone, TV, minibar, radio, hairdrier
Facilities 2 dining-rooms, 2 sitting-rooms, TV room, games room; swimming-pool
Credit cards AE, DC, V
Children welcome; play area
Disabled ground-floor rooms; lift/elevator
Pets accepted in bedrooms
Closed never
Manager Antonio Garcia Barragan

Castellón/Valencia

Hotel Benedicto XIII

The setting of this hotel is not ideal – some way out of Peñíscola towards the N340, on a private villa development. But the atmosphere is quiet and respectable, the staff attentive, and the terrace gardens and pool help to make up for it. Also there is a fine view of the old city, particularly from the dining-room – large and formal, with flowers on the tables – where you can enjoy good ingredients, simply but well prepared, and in plenty. Bedrooms are Castille-style, with matching blankets and curtains, and bamboo chairs on the balconies. The salon sofas are the only serious lapse in taste.

Nearby Peñíscola, (1.5 km).

Las Atalayas, 12598, Peñíscola, Castellón
Tel (964) 480801
Location on hill just out of town; with garden and car parking
Meals breakfast, lunch, dinner
Prices rooms 4,300-6,600pts; breakfast 500pts, dinner 1,700pts
Rooms 28 double, 2 single, one suite, all with bath; all rooms have central heating, phone, TV
Facilities dining-room, sitting-room, bar; swimming-pool, tennis court, table tennis
Credit cards AE, DC, MC, V
Children welcome; games available
Disabled access easy
Pets not accepted
Closed Jan and Feb
Manager Idelfonso Llopis Pau

Hotel Excelsior

Handsome, old and mostly refurbished, the Excelsior offers greater comfort and charm than many of Valencia's more expensive hotels. Despite the odd plastic plant, the whole place is imbued with past elegance: the stairs are carpeted, the lift has brass doors and old furniture is scattered here and there. Many of the bedrooms are let down by their small bathrooms with old fittings, but the suites, with their brass bedsteads, painted cornices, floral textiles and cosy ante-rooms, are highly desirable. Away from your room, you have to choose between a noisy bar and a somewhat formal English-style sitting-room.

Nearby Palacio del Marqués de Dos Aguas, Lonja, market.

Calle Barcelonina 5, 46002, Valencia
Tel (96) 514612
Location in middle of town, near Plaza del Ayuntamiento; no private car parking
Meals breakfast, lunch, dinner
Prices rooms 6,350-12,600pts; breakfast 500pts, lunch 1,150pts, dinner 1,450pts
Rooms 38 double, 18 single, 9 family rooms, all with bath; all rooms have central heating, air-conditioning, phone; most rooms have TV
Facilities dining-room, sitting-room, cafeteria
Credit cards AE, DC, MC, V
Children welcome
Disabled easy access; lift/elevator
Pets not accepted
Closed never
Manager Roberto Plá

Alicante

Hotels on the Costa Blanca

For many visitors, the Costa Blanca is synonymous with Benidorm, where tower blocks form a wall behind one of Spain's grandest beaches. But up the coast at Calpe we found some hotels worth an entry here, and there are a few others that are worth a mention.

Just inland from Benidorm, for example, is the tiny town of Alfaz del Pi, which enjoys the double distinctions of being twinned with Oslo and holding an excellent annual film festival; the 10-room El Moli is a pleasant and cheap place to stay (Tel (96) 588 8244).

Down the coast a little way is Villajoyosa, where the smart Montíboli, built in Moorish style with a central patio, enjoys a privileged setting on a promontory; the pool is reportedly 'beautiful' and the 50 rooms well decorated, 'with individual themes' (Tel (96) 589 0250).

The remarkable palm groves of Elche are only a few miles inland from Alicante, at the southern extremity of the Costa Blanca. The 70-room Huerto del Cura is an exceptionally civilized hotel, and the obvious place to stay in Elche if you can afford its highish prices: it is set amid palm trees just across the road from the famous, riotously colourful gardens of the same name. The hotel is a 'Parador colaborador', meaning that it shares some of the marketing arrangements of the state-run chain (Tel (96) 545 8040).

Hotel Palas

Located at one end of Alicante's attractive, palm-lined promenade, running along the harbour, the Palas has a delicious feeling of turn-of-the-century decaying grandeur about it. Which means, on the other hand, that it does not yield all creature comforts and mod. cons. The ground floor, dominated by dark wooden furniture and fittings, and hung throughout with paintings in a variety of styles, is busy with life. The dining-room/restaurant is large, well-lit and renowned for its pasta dishes. At the back of the hotel a modern extension includes a pleasant café area with white wicker chairs as well as a nondescript TV room.
Nearby Beach, old quarter and lift to castle; Elche (24km).

Calle Cervantes 5, 03002, Alicante
Tel (96) 520 9211
Location near entrance to port, on Explanada; with car parking
Meals breakfast, lunch, dinner
Prices rooms 4,460-8,825pts; breakfast 500pts, menus 1,800-2,000pts; children's menu available
Rooms 30 double, 17 single, all with bath; all rooms have central heating, phone
Facilities 2 dining-rooms, sitting-room
Credit cards AE, DC, MC, V
Children welcome
Disabled access easy; lift/elevator
Pets accepted in bedrooms
Closed November
Proprietor Pedro Creixell

Alicante

Roadside inn, Calpe

Venta La Chata

It is easy to imagine coaches drawing up at this old inn a hundred years ago to change horses and set down passengers for the night. Since then it has been restored and partly modernized, keeping the old flavour but adding some of the comforts that modern travellers expect.

The rooms are varied, mixing old and new furniture in a piecemeal assortment. Most of the bathrooms have ageing fittings. Ask for a room with a terrace-suntrap overlooking the leafy, peaceful garden. Some of the rooms also have views of Calpe's Gibraltar-like rock, the Peñón de Ifach.

Downstairs there are informal tables in the breakfast/TV room in front of reception and more inviting chairs and tables on the two terraces and under the arches of the entrance porch. The cool, open-plan sitting-room, decorated with old pots, gourds and an enormous gold-framed mirror, has some cosy armchairs. The restaurant, popular with non-residents, is lit by a long line of windows and has a door leading into the garden. Among the cactuses, clumps of bamboo and flowers that gather around a mature carob tree, there are some quiet, shady corners.

Nearby Calpe (5 km), Peñón de Ifach (10km), Altea (15 km), Jávea (25 km), Castell de Guadalest (35 km).

Carretera de Valencia, 03710, Calpe, Alicante
Tel (96) 583 0308
Location on main N332 (Valencia to Alicante), just outside Calpe; with garden and car parking
Meals breakfast, lunch, dinner
Prices rooms 1,950-3,900pts; breakfast 340pts, dinner 900-1,599pts
Rooms 16 double, 1 single, all with bath; all rooms have central heating, phone
Facilities dining-room, 2 sitting-rooms, terrace; tennis court
Credit cards AE, DC, V
Children welcome; play area in garden
Disabled access difficult
Pets accepted
Closed mid-Nov to mid-Dec
Proprietor Hermanos Giner

Alicante

Seaside hotel, Calpe

Paradero de Ifach

In a commanding position above the beach next to Calpe's fishing harbour, and at the foot of the great rock after which the hotel is named, the Paradero de Ifach has inadvertently conserved much of its original 1930s atmosphere. Its owners have not tried to keep it as it was: they have simply left it alone.

The interior charm of the hotel is mainly downstairs. The sitting-room has a semicircle of windows giving wide views of the sea and the coast southwards. The breakfast room also has large windows, and a ceiling completely clad in living ivy. From the wide sunny terrace outside, a path zig-zags down to the sand immediately below.

The bedrooms – old, sparsely furnished and little improved – are not the strong point of the place. The doors sometimes stick and the tiled floors can be uneven and bumpy. But nine of them have large private balconies with chairs and tables overlooking the sandy beach.

This hotel may be neglected in parts, but it is more relaxing than many expensive seaside hotels where the furnishings have been planned down to the last detail.

Nearby Peñon de Ifach (an hour's walk to the top); Altea (15 km); Benidorm (25 km); Guadalest (30 km).

Explanada del Puerto, 03710, Calpe, Alicante
Tel (96) 5830300
Location at foot of looming rock near port, overlooking harbour and beach; with car parking
Meals breakfast
Prices rooms 2,475-4,950pts; breakfast 300pts
Rooms 12 double, 17 single, all with bath; all rooms have phone

Facilities dining-room, sitting-room, bar/breakfast room, terrace
Credit cards AE, DC, MC, V
Children welcome
Disabled access not possible
Pets accepted
Closed Nov to Mar
Proprietor Pilar Garcia Vives

Alicante

Hotel Mediterraneo

A short way back from the sea-front of a developing resort, this recently opened, family-run hotel has been carefully decorated throughout, from its black marble steps and white balustrades to its interior colour schemes. It is all modern and harmonious, but perhaps a little over-designed in places, with an excess of brass and glass details. The bedrooms are light and brightly painted, with smart bathrooms and pleasant balconies. A covered roof-top terrace lounge is to be added to the building shortly. It is a particularly relaxing place in winter, when the resort is dormant.

Nearby Las Dunas (1 km) – wooded dunes; Elche (30 km).

Avenida Cartagena, 03140, Guardamar del Segura, Alicante
Tel (96) 5729407
Location in developing part of resort, two minutes from beach; with car parking
Meals breakfast, lunch, dinner
Prices rooms 2,090-4,620pts; breakfast 350pts, dinner 1,000pts
Rooms 24 double, 8 single, all with bath; all rooms have central heating, phone, minibar
Facilities dining-room, sitting/TV room
Credit cards AE, V
Children welcome
Disabled lift/elevator
Pets not accepted
Closed never
Proprietor Concepción Martinez Cases

Paradores in Eastern Spain

The Paradores on the east coast of Spain are modern and functional, with little charm. The PN Costa del Azahar at Benicarlo is a box-like building (108 rooms) set in beautiful gardens facing 6 km of gently curving beach (Tel (964) 470100). Just south of Valencia, on the narrow sandy peninsula of El Saler is the PN Luis Vives, a golf hotel with its own 18-hole course (Tel (96) 161 1186). Further down the coast on the Javea peninsula is another unremarkable 1960s creation, the 65-room PN Costa Blanca (Tel (965) 790200). The PN de Puerto Lumbreras, 80 km SW of Murcia, is not on the coast, despite its maritime-sounding name. It is a plain but smart white hotel (60 rooms) on the main road through the town. Its floors are chequered marble, and the walls are brightened up by local ceramics (Tel (968) 402025).

Of the places further inland, only the PN La Concordia at Alcañiz (a hilltop castle with just 12 rooms) gets a full entry here (see page 126). The PN de Teruel is a modern hotel overlooking the city which is famous for its integration of Christian, Jewish and Muslim styles of architecture (Tel (974) 602553). The PN de la Mancha, south of Albacete, is a low white building on the sprawling plains of La Mancha. It is decorated in rustic style with beamed ceilings and primitive wooden farm tools hanging from the walls – donkey baskets, oxen yokes, ploughshares (Tel (967) 229450).

Murcia

Spa hotel, Los Alcazares

Balneario La Encarnación

The first and still the finest hotel on Spain's landlocked sea, the Mar Menor, La Encarnación was built in the 1900s at the whim of a wealthy local miner. Ostensibly it is a spa but, despite the evocative marble baths and lead pipes on the ground floor, it merely serves up heated sea water.

One look at the attractive courtyard, dripping with flowers and foliage, its great doors between the double flights of stairs open to the sea, and you will probably forgive the hotel its shortcomings. Francisca Paredes, a jovial businesswoman who is as proud of her family inheritance as she is devoted to her guests, is the first to admit that the high-ceilinged bedrooms upstairs are spartan and rather nondescript. But her regular summer guests – some of whom have been coming for years – put up with the lack of comforts for the lively, welcoming atmosphere; they are entertained with concerts, dances and dinner parties.

There has to be a catch. The hotel is so popular with its regulars – and is open for such a short season – that it is well-nigh impossible to get a room. If you try, go for the beginning or the end of the season and book at least a year in advance.

Nearby Cartagena (25 km), La Manga (30 km), Murcia.

Calle Condesa 1, 30710, Los Alcazares, Murcia
Tel (968) 575004
Location behind beach, off main road through town; with small car park
Meals breakfast, lunch, dinner
Prices rooms FB 4,730-9,200pts
Rooms 15 double, 18 single, 4 family rooms, all with bath
Facilities dining-room, sitting-room, bar, patio
Credit cards AE, DC, MC, V

Children welcome
Disabled access difficult
Pets accepted in bedrooms
Closed Oct to May
Proprietor Francisca Paredes

Murcia

Hotel Conde de Floridablanca

Although built relatively recently, the Conde de Floridablanca has a comforting historical feel. The ground floor is illuminated by large areas of repetitive white-and-yellow stained glass and is decorated with numerous antiques and craft objects. Attention to detail even extends to the lavatories, where there are elegant copper basins. The bedrooms – each named after a town in the province and unpretentiously decorated – are less inspiring but comfortable. You can eat from a hearty menu in the small restaurant at a surprisingly reasonable price.

Nearby Casino and Cathedral, within walking distance; Alcantarilla waterwheel (10 km); Orihuela (27 km).

Calle Princesa 18, 30002, Murcia
Tel (968) 214626
Location in narrow street, on far side of river from city centre; with car parking
Meals breakfast, lunch, dinner
Prices rooms 9,750-11,000pts; breakfast 725pts, dinner 1,000pts
Rooms 73 double, 12 single, all with bath; all rooms have central heating, air-conditioning, phone, TV, minibar, radio
Facilities dining-room, TV/sitting-room, bar
Credit cards AE, DC, MC, V
Children welcome
Disabled easy access; lift/elevator
Pets not accepted
Closed never
Proprietor Angel Imbernon

Hotel Termas

The oldest and most attractive of the three hotels in a leafy spa founded by the Romans, the Termas is decorated inside in a superb Mozarabic style. With its cupolas, patios and ornate plasterwork, at times you could believe that you were staying in the Alhambra. Most guests come for the waters, and there is a rest-cure calm in the sitting-room with its coffered ceiling and card tables. The bedrooms are pleasantly modern, some of them looking through eucalyptus trees to the river. Two floors down is a labyrinth of humid tunnels heated by warm water which gushes out of the ground.

Nearby Murcia (25 km); Alcantarilla waterwheel (30 km).

Balneario de Archena, 30600, Archena, Murcia
Tel (968) 670100
Location by river Segura, through town (follow signs); with grounds and car parking
Meals breakfast, lunch, dinner
Prices rooms 6,700-8,400pts; breakfast 600pts, dinner 2,050pts
Rooms 60 double, 10 single, all with bath; all have central heating, air-conditioning, phone, minibar, radio
Facilities dining-room, sitting-room, 2 TV rooms, spa; swimming-pool, 2 tennis courts
Credit cards not accepted
Children welcome
Disabled easy access; lift/elevator
Pets not accepted
Closed never
Manager Miguel Lloret Perez

Huelva

Country hotel, Los Marines

Finca Buenvino

As our inspectors discovered, this is not an easy place to find; the lovely modern villa, built in 18thC style on the top of a hill, is hidden away in the heart of a National Park, amid chestnut forests, fruit trees and bubbling springs.

Sam and Jeannie Chesterton, an English couple, stress that this is their home and that you are expected to join in with the family (who are very easy-going). Everyone eats together – on the terrace in summer or in the panelled dining-room. Jeannie is a trained cordon bleu cook, and produces mouth-watering dinners and salad lunches, accompanied by liberal amounts of wine. Drinks taken at other times – and perhaps consumed before the huge fireplace of the sitting-room or in the airy conservatory – are recorded in an 'honesty book'.

The bedrooms are all bright and comfortable. The two attic rooms have hand-stencilled walls and wonderful views over the woods. The other two rooms are smaller and share a bathroom. The Chestertons are planning to restore the cottages on their land for further guests, who will also dine at the house and have use of the swimming-pool, spectacularly perched above the house.

Nearby Aracena (caves and castle); Zafra (85 km).

21293, Los Marines, Huelva
Tel (955) 124034
Location in heart of woodland, off N433 W of Los Marines, itself W of Aracena; with garden and shaded car parking
Meals breakfast, lunch, dinner
Prices DB&B 10,000-12,000pts
Rooms 4 double, 2 with bath; all rooms have central heating
Facilities dining-room, sitting-room, TV room, conservatory; swimming-pool
Credit cards not accepted
Children welcome; play facilities
Disabled access difficult
Pets tolerated if necessary
Closed Christmas
Proprietors Sam and Jeannie Chesterton

Huelva

Town hotel, Aracena

Sierra de Aracena

The attractive town of Aracena is built in tiers on a hillside crowned by the remains of a Templar's castle. Beneath it, underground rivers have carved out vast narrow caves full of spectacular formations, coloured red by iron oxide – well worth exploring if you are passing through the region.

The Sierra de Aracena, in the wide, cobbled Gran Vía, makes a good base for an overnight stay. It is a solid, square building with an elaborate brick-patterned façade and arches around the ground-floor windows. It is a quiet, sleepy hotel, where the world drifts by without intruding; a few locals may wander in to watch the TV. The sitting-room is pleasantly furnished with wicker chairs, floral fabrics and tiled pictures, and adjoins a modern bar (which doubles as a breakfast room). There is an open fire in winter.

The bedrooms are simple and comfortable. The ones at the back have great views of the castle and Aracena's winding streets and red-tiled roofs. They are all kept spotlessly clean by the friendly staff, who don't speak a word of English but seldom stop smiling. There is no dining-room but several recommended restaurants are to be found in the town.

Nearby Cave of Marvels, castle; Zafra (95 km).

Gran Via 21, 21200, Aracena, Huelva
Tel (955) 110775
Location on quiet wide street in middle of town; with parking for 8 cars
Meals breakfast
Prices rooms 2,600-6,500pts; breakfast 150-300pts
Rooms 27 double, 9 single, 2 suites, all with bath; all rooms have central heating, phone, radio; some rooms have TV and minibar
Facilities sitting-room, bar/breakfast area
Credit cards V
Children accepted
Disabled lift/elevator; some ground-floor rooms
Pets not accepted
Closed never
Manager Antonio Campos Dominguez

Seville

Castle Parador, Carmona

PN Alcázar del Rey Don Pedro

With 65 rooms and conference facilities, this Parador can hardly be described as 'small and charming'. But it merits inclusion because of its superb location on a hill top above the busy walled town of Carmona. The views are breath-taking.

The Moorish fortress that stood here was transformed into a luxury palace by the craftsmen of the Seville Alcázar for the infamous Don Pedro the Cruel. The Parador architects have taken great care to recreate the 'palace' atmosphere, setting elegant Mudejar columns around a pretty internal courtyard and decorating the stonework and floor tiles with the familiar Moorish star pattern.

The public rooms are large and comfortable; glass cases of swords and armour and hanging tapestries give them a 'stately home' feel, but on our visit both the sitting-rooms and cavernous dining-room seemed positively animated. Top-floor bedrooms have amazing views over the fertile plains of the Corbones river. The rooms are comfortable and show more attention to detail than the average Parador room (we had great trouble locating the disguised minibar).

Nearby Roman remains; Seville (35 km), Ecija (55 km) – palaces and churches; Córdoba (105 km).

41410, Carmona, Seville
Tel (95) 414 1010
Location on top of hill in Carmona (follow Parador signs); with garden and ample shaded car parking
Meals breakfast, lunch, dinner
Prices rooms 17,000-25,000pts, breakfast 1,200 pts, dinner 3,500pts
Rooms 57 double, 8 single, all with bath; all rooms have central heating,

air-conditioning, phone, TV, hairdrier, minibar, radio
Facilities dining-room, 2 sitting-rooms, bar; swimming-pool
Credit cards AE, DC, V
Children welcome
Disabled most rooms are on ground floor
Pets not accepted
Closed never
Manager Benito Montanes Sierra

Seville

Town house hotel, Seville

Hotel Simon

Don't be put off by the neon sign outside; once inside the white wrought iron gates, you find yourself transported back in time. Behind them is the typical Andalucian courtyard of a beautiful Moorish town house – a perfect place to cool down among the ferns and marble busts after a busy morning's sightseeing in this spectacular town.

The hotel's dining-room is reminiscent of a mosque; the walls are covered in pretty Moorish tiles and gilded mirrors. Glass chandeliers hang down between the slender marble pillars. The stairway and corridors are decorated in a similar style, with tiled walls and floors, period furniture and cabinets full of silver. Bedrooms tend to vary in size and quality and are the original rooms of this lovely 18thC house. Some have small balconies looking on to the street, while others are rather small and airless. Bathrooms also vary, but all are spotlessly clean.

The staff are friendly and helpful, and obviously take great pride in this unusual hotel. The Simon has only one minor disadvantage – no car parking immediately outside. But it is possible to park your car nearby and this drawback is certainly outweighed by the hotel's attractions.

Nearby Cathedral, La Giralda, the Alcázar, Jewish quarter.

García de Vinuesa 19, 41001, Seville
Tel (95) 226660
Location on small street, just west of cathedral; no private car parking
Meals breakfast, lunch, dinner
Prices rooms 4,300-9,000pts; breakfast 300pts, lunch and dinner 1,750pts
Rooms 27 double, 13 with bath, 7 with shower; 13 single, 5 with shower; 6 family, 3 with bath, 3 with shower; all rooms have central heating, phone
Facilities dining-room, sitting-room, patio
Credit cards AE, DC, MC, V
Children accepted
Disabled some ground-floor rooms
Pets accepted in bedrooms
Closed never
Proprietor Francisca García Canet

Seville

Town house hotel, Seville

Hotel Doña Maria

Imagine lying by a swimming-pool which overlooks one of the biggest cathedrals in the world – just one of the perks of staying at the Doña Maria in the heart of Seville. The hotel is built in an old town house, in a cobbled alley-way off the cathedral square – very convenient for sightseeing, not so convenient for parking, unless you get a space in the underground car park.

The hotel has no dining-room, but serves large buffet breakfasts downstairs, and has two bars – one wood-panelled, adjoining the sitting-room, the other on the roof-terrace (in summer only). The other public rooms are elegant and comfortable – the sitting-room has dark red sofas between brick pillars, the landings are crammed with antiques and portraits, the corridors are lit with blue and white glass lamps; and there is a tiny tropical garden in the middle of the building.

Each bedroom is different, apparently decorated by the Marchioness de San Joaquin herself and named after eminent Sevillian ladies. If possible, ask to see several rooms and choose carefully, as some are disappointing and not cheap. The roof-terrace certainly makes up for it – there are not many places where you get a view of Gothic spires as you swim.

Nearby Cathedral, La Giralda, the Alcázar, Jewish quarter.

Don Remondo 19, 41004, Seville
Tel (95) 422 4990
Location in narrow alley-way, leading from square in front of cathedral; underground parking for 9 cars
Meals breakfast
Prices rooms 12,000-17,000pts; breakfast 650pts
Rooms 35 double, all with bath; 14 single, 12 with bath, 3 with shower; all rooms have central heating, air-conditioning, phone, TV, radio; swimming-pool on roof
Facilities 2 sitting-rooms, bar, breakfast room
Credit cards AE, DC, MC, V
Children welcome
Disabled lift/elevator
Pets accepted in 2 bedrooms
Closed never
Proprietor Federico Garcia Corona

Seville

Town house hotel, Seville

Hotel Murillo

To find the Hotel Murillo you need a good sense of direction and a detailed map; it is lost in the historic Barrio de Santa Cruz, a maze of tiny pedestrian passages behind the Alcázar. From the outside, it is a typical Sevillian town house, painted mustard-yellow and white, with wrought-iron grilles and balconies.

From the inside, it is an extraordinary place, a treasure trove of peculiar objects and antiques. Suits of armour guard the entrance to a long, dim room crammed with furniture – leather sling chairs around carved tables, elaborate screens and glass cabinets along the walls, a sedan chair in front of the bar. The panelled ceiling gives you the feeling that you are in the cabin of a medieval ship. This room serves as a sitting, eating and reception area, and there is another small sitting-room for families or groups.

In contrast, the bedrooms upstairs are rather plain. Second-floor rooms have small balconies looking on to the street, third-floor rooms have arched windows. Furniture is functional and bathrooms small. The room keys are attached to miniature paint pallets, emphasizing the connection with the Sevillian artist Murillo, after whom the hotel is named.

Nearby Cathedral, La Giralda, the Alcázar, Jewish quarter.

Lope de Rueda 7 & 9, 41000, Seville
Tel (95) 421 6095
Location in a maze of tiny streets, north of cathedral, approachable only by foot; garages nearby
Meals breakfast
Prices rooms 8,000-14,500pts; breakfast 300pts
Rooms 8 double, all with bath; 9 single, with bath,; all rooms have central heating, air-conditioning, phone
Facilities sitting-room, bar
Credit cards AE, DC, MC, V
Children accepted
Disabled lift/elevator
Pets not accepted
Closed never
Manager Miguel-Angel Adarve

Seville

Andalucian villa, Alcalá de Guadaira

Hotel Oromana

Our inspector had trouble finding the Oromana; it is on a hill opposite the town, in an area (of the same name) which is rapidly being developed for residential purposes, eating into the pine woods that surround the hotel. The tranquillity is not yet lost; a long winding drive takes you away from the building sites to the rounded knoll where this impressive white hotel, complete with bell-tower, overlooks the meandering Guadaira river.

There is a particularly Spanish feel to the lofty public rooms; reception leads into a vaulted sitting-room of marble columns and ornamental Spanish vases. Its large French windows open on to a bougainvillaea-clad terrace where guests can sit and enjoy the view. Next door is a small cosy bar, serving *tapas* at red-and-white checked tables. The more formal dark green dining-room has fresh flowers on every table and sombre pictures of matadors on the walls. All service comes with a smile.

The bedrooms, decorated in the same dark green as the dining-room, are in the main building and in a new extension which overlooks the swimming-pool and beds of roses and lilies. The rooms vary in size but not quality. Some have balconies – a welcome extra in the heat of the Andalucian summer.

Nearby Seville (15 km) – cathedral and palaces.

Avenida de Portugal, 41500, Alcalá de Guadaira, Seville
Tel (95) 470 0804
Location amid pine trees, on hill overlooking town and river; with gardens and ample car parking
Meals breakfast, lunch, dinner
Prices B&B 9,600-12,000pts; breakfast 600, dinner 2,800pts
Rooms 26 doubles, 3 family rooms; all with bath; all rooms have central heating, air-conditioning, phone, TV
Facilities dining-room, 2 sitting-rooms, bar/cafeteria, terrace; swimming-pool
Credit cards AE, DC, V
Children welcome
Disabled lift/elevator
Pets not accepted
Closed never
Manager Peter Opasky

Córdoba

Town house hotel, Córdoba

Hotel González

Hidden away in one of the narrow, white-washed streets in Córdoba's old Jewish quarter, just a stone's throw from the beautiful Mezquita, is this unusual little hotel, built in the remains of a 16thC Moorish palace and so far (we believe) undiscovered by other guidebooks. The only remaining 'remains' we could see were the rectangular stone doorway and one stone capital, but Joaquin and Manuel Gonzalez have added plenty of Moorish touches, such as arabesque arches on the patio. They also run a souvenir shop adjoining the hotel, full of gaudy Moorish vases, but this does not affect (or reflect) the character of the hotel, which is run with a happy blend of informality and efficiency.

Our first impression was of a cool marble interior and a charming receptionist. The hall leads through the arches to a lovely patio, packed with pretty red and white dining-tables and copious flowers and greenery. Geraniums hang down from every possible ledge and balcony. There is also a modern bar where breakfast is served, and a rather dim sitting-room full of antique oil paintings. Upstairs, the bedrooms are simple and comfortable; most have small balconies looking over the patio.

Nearby Mezquita, Alcázar, old Jewish quarter.

Manriquez 3, 14003, Córdoba	air-conditioning, phone, radio
Tel (957) 479819	**Facilities** dining-room/patio,
Location in quiet street	sitting-room, cafeteria/bar,
behind Mezquita (best found	souvenir shop
on foot); no private car	**Credit cards** AE, DC, MC, V
parking – public car park	**Children** welcome
nearby	**Disabled** no special facilities
Meals breakfast, lunch, dinner	**Pets** not accepted
Prices rooms 4,450-8,460pts;	**Closed** restaurant only Nov
breakfast 450pts,	**Proprietor** Joaquin and
Rooms 15 double, 2 single, all	Manuel Gonzalez
with bath; all rooms have	
central heating,	

Córdoba

Town hotel, Cordoba

Hotel Albucasis

We came upon this hotel, hidden in a quiet courtyard in the old Jewish quarter, completely by chance. It is only a couple of streets behind the Mezquita – close enough to walk there in minutes, yet far enough away to escape the souvenir shops and bus-loads of tourists. The only indication of a hotel is a two-star sign outside an archway, leading into a stone-flagged courtyard. Ivy and apricot trees grow up the white, four-storey building inside the courtyard. You can sit out under the trees at iron tables and chairs, or relax in air-conditioned luxury on the other side of the French windows.

The interior is smart and new, tell-tale signs that the hotel was built only a couple of years ago. The main room doubles as a bar and breakfast area; it is a happy blend of old and new – modern furniture offset by old pistols and swords on the walls and an ancient wrought iron lamp in the middle of the room. Magazines and vases of fresh carnations add home-like touches.

The bedrooms are also smart and spotless, decorated in green and white. Most look on to the courtyard – those on the other side are smaller and have tiny bathrooms.

Nearby Mezquita, Alcázar, old Jewish quarter, archaeological museum.

Buen Pastor 11, 14003, Córdoba
Tel (957) 478625
Location in old Jewish quarter, 5 minutes walk from the Mezquita; no private car parking
Meals breakfast
Prices rooms 5,500-8,500pts; breakfast 500pts
Rooms 9 double, 6 single, all with bath; all rooms have central heating, air-conditioning, phone; some rooms have TV
Facilities bar/sitting-room/breakfast room, terrace
Credit cards V
Children tolerated
Disabled access easy, lift/elevator
Pets not accepted
Closed never
Manager Alfonso Salas Camacho

Córdoba

Hotel Marisa

If you are looking for a convenient location in downtown Córdoba, you are unlikely to find anything to beat the Marisa, an attractive white town house directly opposite the entrance to the Mesquita.

It is a pleasant, inexpensive hotel with spotless modern bedrooms and a large cool sitting-area and breakfast bar, looking on to a tiny cobbled patio full of ferns. The simplicity of the decoration – white walls with black iron torch-holders, chequered floor-tiles – reflects the nature of the hotel; functional but not without a certain style.

Nearby Mesquita, Alcazar, old Jewish quarter.

Cardenal Herrero 6, 14003, Córdoba
Tel (957) 473142
Location opposite entrance to Mesquita; car parking nearby
Meals breakfast
Prices rooms 5,600-6,300pts; breakfast 425pts
Rooms 23 double, 10 with shower, 13 with bath; 5 single, all with bath; all rooms have central heating, air-conditioning, phone
Facilities sitting/breakfast room
Credit cards AE, MC, V
Children accepted
Disabled no special facilities
Pets not accepted
Closed never
Manager Rafael Sanz Coll

Paradores in Andalucía

The two Paradores in Huelva are both modern. The 53-room PN Costa de la Luz at Ayamonte, on the borders of Portugal, is a sprawling white building high above the city, with magnificent views (Tel (955) 320700). The 43-room PN Cristóbal Colón is on the coast, just beyond Mazágon; a footpath goes down to a sandy beach (Tel (955) 376000). Cádiz has a large modern Parador, a six-storey white complex called the Atlántico, on the south side of the isthmus. Ask for a room with a sea view (Tel (956) 226905).

The Costa del Sol has three Paradores. Two are close to Málaga – as well as the PN de Gibralfaro (see page 169) there is the self-explanatory Golf, a little way west of the town (Tel (952) 381255). The third is at Nerja: large and modern but attractive, with well-furnished rooms and an elevator down to the beach (Tel (952) 520050). North-east of Almería is PN Reyes Católicos at Mojácar (see page 156).

Inland, the Paradores at Antequera, Arcos de la Frontera, Carmona, Granada, Jaén, Sierra Nevada and Úbeda have detailed entries. The modern 83-room PN de la Arruzafa at Córdoba is 3 km from the middle of the city (Tel (957) 275900). The dismal PN de Bailén has little to recommend it apart from its pool (Tel (953) 670100). Much more appealing is the PN El Adelantado at Cazorla – a simple, attractive mountain lodge in the wild Sierra de Segura, popular in the autumn (Tel (953) 721075).

Córdoba

Converted monastery, Palma del Rio

Hospedería de San Francisco

This 15thC Franciscan monastery stands on a small square at the centre of a confusing one-way system. If you get lost, don't hesitate to ask for directions; everyone knows where the Hospedería is, as it becomes a focus of attention at fiesta time (the staff dress up as monks and run a bar behind the church).

The Moreno family converted the monastery into a hotel five years ago. The care they took is immediately obvious as you enter the main courtyard; tables are set up in the cloisters, where you can watch pigeons nesting in the bell-tower as you eat. The main dining-room is a high-ceilinged hall, dominated by a huge fireplace. All the sitting areas are comfortable, especially the tiled bar, with its beamed ceiling and old paintings. Some of the bedrooms were once monks' cells and are fairly small and basic, but what they lack in luxuries they make up for in character, with beautifully hand-painted basins and bed-covers woven by local nuns. Ten new bedrooms were being added in 1990.

Chef Iñaki has an excellent reputation, and his caricature (round, moustached and wagging a long finger) adorns the constantly changing menu, which reflects his Basque origins.

Nearby Córdoba (55 km); Seville (90 km); churches and palaces in Écija and Carmona.

Avenida Pio X11, 14700, Palma del Rio, Córdoba
Tel (957) 710732
Location on quiet square in heart of town; with car parking on street
Meals breakfast, lunch, dinner
Prices rooms 8,000-20,000pts; breakfast 650pts, lunch 2,450pts, dinner 2,250pts
Rooms 9 double, all with bath; all rooms have central heating, air-conditioning,

phone
Facilities 2 dining-rooms, sitting-room, bar, patio
Credit cards V
Children welcome
Disabled no special facilities
Pets not accepted
Closed restaurant only, Sun dinner, and Sun lunch in Jul and Aug
Manager Iñaki Martinez Gonzalez

Jaén

Town mansion, Úbeda

PN Condestable Dávalos

Somewhat overshadowed by the lovely façade of the 16thC chapel next door to it, Úbeda's stately Parador stands on the Renaissance square of Vázquez de Molina. Its internal courtyard is delightful; sixteen slender pillars (on both floors) enclose a stone-flagged patio set with tables and chairs. Striking blue-and-white patterned tiles half cover the walls around the outside. A sweeping staircase leads to the glass-enclosed gallery, past suits of armour and a spectacular light inside a double-headed glass eagle. Some bedrooms are around the gallery, others look on to smaller leafy quads or the ornamental garden. There is more attention to detail here than in the average Parador – carved bed-heads, hand-painted mirrors and wooden writing desks.

Guests have the choice of two bars, the underground taberna or a bar-cum-sitting-room on the way to the gardens. Red-tiled floors with little picture inlays are found in all public rooms, including the attractive dining-room. It is a friendly and animated place, in which it is easy to relax – perhaps in the shade of giant ferns in the courtyard, or under pine trees in the garden. It seemed half the size of its 31 rooms, without being cramped – a great base for exploring this historic town.

Nearby Plaza, palaces, churches; Baeza (10 km); Jaén (55 km).

Plaza de Vásquez de Molina 1, 23400, Ubeda, Jaén
Tel (953) 750345
Location on square in historic part of town; follow signs; with car parking
Meals breakfast, lunch, dinner
Prices rooms 12,000-14,000pts; breakfast 1,100pts, dinner 3,200pts
Rooms 31 double, all with bath; all rooms have central heating, air-conditioning, phone, TV, minibar, hairdrier, radio
Facilities 2 dining-rooms, sitting-room, TV room, bar, cafeteria
Credit cards AE, DC, MC, V
Children welcome
Disabled access difficult
Pets not accepted, except guide dogs
Closed never
Manager José Maria Ronda

Jaén

Castle Parador, Jaén

PN Castillo de Santa Catalina

A small road zig-zags up the pine-clad hill behind the busy town of Jaén to this spectacular Parador perched on a rocky promontory. It is a stark, modern fortress, built next to a Moorish Alcazar. The views are breath-taking; to the west the patchwork plains of the Guadalquivir, to the east the craggy Sierra Morena.

The Parador has been constructed with infinite care to create a castle-like atmosphere – corridors are dimly lit, windows are small and arched, doors are huge with heavy bolts, rooms are cavernous and decorated with banners and tapestries. The reception leads to an echoing split-level sitting-room with a secret passage leading to the roof. At the opposite end of the building is the magnificent domed salon cupula – brick arches cross at a point about 70 feet above your head and sunlight filters through huge star-studded shutters. The room opens on to an arched dining-room, with high-backed chairs.

In contrast, the sleeping quarters are light and airy – bedrooms and corridors have whitewashed walls bordered with pretty green tiles. The rooms are comfortable, and some have balconies with stunning views of the mountains. A triangular stairway leads to the gardens and swimming-pool.

Nearby cathedral; Úbeda (55 km); Córdoba (110 km).

Carretera del Castillo, 23000, Jaén
Tel (953) 264411
Location on hill overlooking town; with car parking
Meals breakfast, lunch, dinner
Prices rooms 11,000-12,500pts; breakfast 1,100pts, dinner 3,200pts
Rooms 45 double, all with bath; all rooms have central heating, air-conditioning, phone, TV, minibar

Facilities dining-room, 2 sitting-rooms, bar; swimming-pool
Credit cards AE, DC, MC, V
Children accepted
Disabled access easy; ground-floor rooms; lift/elevator
Pets not accepted
Closed never
Manager Antonio Romero Huete

Granada

Hotel América

Tucked away between the Alhambra and Granada's Parador (page 152), this delightful family-run hotel offers a perfect location at an affordable price. It is a small, friendly place, built around a vine-covered patio. In the summer months, the patio doubles as a dining-room – pretty tiled tables are set out, and you dine by the light of hanging lanterns to the sound of running water. The choice of dishes is limited, but everything is home-cooked, and if the smells coming from the kitchen when we visited are anything to go by, the food is delicious; it is also reasonably priced.

The bedrooms are small but comfortable and clean, and overlook either the patio or the gardens of the Alhambra. They are brightened up by colourful woven bedspreads and curtains. The sitting area next to the reception is crammed with pottery, ornaments, screens, sofas and rocking chairs – leaving hardly enough room to sit down. It is a small, busy hotel, and not the kind of place you would want to linger in all day. But with the Alhambra on your doorstep, there is more than enough to keep you busy.

Nearby Alhambra, Generalife and gardens, cathedral; Sierra Nevada (35 km), Costa del Sol (65 km).

Real de la Alhambra 53,
18009, Granada
Tel (958) 227471
Location inside walls of
Alhambra (follow road past
entrance); car parking around
square
Meals breakfast, lunch, dinner
Prices rooms 5,500-12,000pts,
breakfast 700pts, dinner
1,800pts
Rooms 8 double, one family
room, all with bath; 4 single, 2

with bath, 2 with shower; all
rooms have central heating,
phone
Facilities dining-room
Credit cards not accepted
Children not accepted
Disabled one ground-floor
room
Pets not accepted
Closed early Nov to Feb
Proprietor Rafael Garzón
Roman

Granada

PN San Francisco

'Book at least three months in advance' was the advice that the management of this extremely popular Parador asked us to pass on; 'and more in high season', we would add. The attraction of this converted 14thC convent, set in the gardens of the famous Alhambra, is easy to see – especially when the day-trippers have disappeared – and the results are predictable.

Although the hotel is rather big and impersonal, it has some lovely touches – the chapel where Isabella of Spain was originally buried, now open to the sky, is used as a patio, and the adjoining courtyard full of plants and flowers is a place to sit and relax in lovely old rocking-chairs. Alcoves in the corridors and stairways are decorated with carved wooden figures of saints, and the stone-flagged floors are covered in bright Granadan rugs. The bedrooms are fairly standard, with large, tiled bathrooms; those numbered in the 200s have superb views over the Alhambra and the Generalife. Public rooms are comfortable, and there are seating areas on the terraces. The dining-room gets very busy – but any hotel near the Alhambra attracts crowds, and at least here you can sit and wait in glorious surroundings.

Nearby Alhambra, Generalife and gardens, cathedral; Sierra Nevada (35 km), Costa del Sol (65 km).

Real de la Alhambra, 18009, Granada
Tel (958) 221440
Location in Alhambra gardens (follow road past entrance); with garden and garage for 17 cars
Meals breakfast, lunch, dinner
Prices rooms 22,000pts; breakfast 1,200pts, dinner 3,500pts
Rooms 35 double, 4 single, all with bath; all rooms have central heating, air-conditioning, phone, TV, minibar, hairdrier
Facilities dining-room, sitting-room, bar
Credit cards AE, DC, MC, V
Children welcome
Disabled some ground-floor rooms
Pets not accepted
Closed never
Manager D Juan Antonio Fernandez Aladro

Granada

Hotel Guadalupe

If all the small hotels on the Alhambra hill are booked up in high season, try this slightly larger hotel run by two brothers – equally convenient and very comfortable. Green and white Moorish tiles border the corridors leading to sizeable bedrooms – some with views over the Alhambra, and some with red-brick balconies. Meals are served in the pink and white dining-room on the second floor, and you can also get snacks in the bar, which doubles as a sitting-room, furnished with paisley sofas, glass coffee tables, card tables and oil paintings. The atmosphere is friendly, and the clientele cosmopolitan.

Nearby Alhambra, Generalife and gardens, cathedral.

Avenida de los Alixares, 18009, Granada
Tel (958) 223423
Location near Alhambra, on road past coach/car park; car parking on street
Meals breakfast, lunch, dinner
Prices rooms 5,400-9,300pts; breakfast 600pts, dinner 1,900pts
Rooms 51 double, 7 single; all with bath; all rooms have central heating, air-conditioning, phone, radio; some rooms have minibar
Facilities dining-room, bar/TV room
Credit cards AE, DC, MC, V
Children welcome
Disabled lift/elevator
Pets accepted in bedrooms
Closed never
Proprietor Carlos and Vida Ma Bocanegra Rodriguez

Reporting to the guide

Please write and tell us about your experiences of small hotels, guest-houses and inns, whether good or bad, whether listed in this edition or not. As well as hotels in Spain, we are interested in hotels in Britain and Ireland, Italy, France, Portugal, Austria, Switzerland, Germany and other European countries, and those in the eastern and western United States.

The address to write to is:
Chris Gill
Charming Small Hotel Guides
The Old Forge
Norton St Philip
Bath BA3 6LW
England

It would be very helpful if you could organize your report under the headings given on page 11. We assume that in writing you have no objections to your views being published unpaid, either verbatim or in an edited version. Names of major outside contributors are acknowledged, at the editor's discretion, in the guide.

If you would be interested in looking at hotels on a professional basis on behalf of the guides, please include on a separate sheet a short CV and a summary of your travel and hotel-going experience.

Granada

Mountain Parador, Sierra Nevada

PN de Sierra Nevada

This is a get-away-from-it-all place, tiered on the mountainside above the winter ski resort of Sierra Nevada (sometimes known by its original name of Sol y Nieve). Although only an hour's drive from Granada, it seems light years away. The scenery is spectacular; as you wind your way almost two thousand metres up the mountain, green valleys give way to sheer cliffs and snow-capped peaks.

The Parador's main purpose is to accommodate skiers from December to May, and it is laid out like a ski chalet and largely furnished in wood – some of which looks scuffed and worn. It is functional rather than noticeably comfortable (if you sink down into the low leather seats in the sitting-room you'll be in for a surprise). Ask for a bedroom with a view down the valley; these have enclosed balconies with window seats. All the rooms have large bathrooms and plenty of hot water.

One of the highlights of a stay here is being able to watch the sun sink below the mountains as you dine. The food and wine are excellent, but the views that go with them are simply sensational. The Parador is also an excellent base for long walks in the mountains.

Nearby skiing, mountain walking; Granada (35 km).

Monachil, 18196, Granada
Tel (958) 480200
Location on mountainside, 35 km from Granada on GR420; with garage
Meals breakfast, lunch, dinner
Prices rooms 9,000pts; breakfast 1,000pts, dinner 3,000pts,
Rooms 32 double, all with bath or shower; all rooms have central heating, phone, TV, minibar

Facilities dining-room, bar/sitting-room, TV/games room
Credit cards AE, DC, MC, V
Children welcome
Disabled no special facilities
Pets not accepted
Closed mid-Oct to mid-Nov
Manager D Salvador Embiz Fabregas

Granada

Converted inn, Gualchos

La Posada

Explore this tiny white village on foot before you attempt to drive to La Posada on the main square – the narrow streets were built for donkeys, not cars. The hotel is set in two houses above a beautiful 'English' garden, with panoramic views of the sea and mountains. It has quite a history; once the home of the village mayor, shot in the Civil War, it was then turned into an inn (hence *La Posada*) before being deserted for some years, and eventually taken on as a holiday home.

In 1985 it was opened as a hotel and restaurant by Bill Job and José Gonzalez. They have restored it beautifully and filled the rooms with collector's items from all over Spain. The bedrooms are all highly individual, with undulating floors, heavy wooden furniture, huge beds, spotless bathrooms and wonderful views. The sitting-room could be in your own home; a fridge serves as an honesty bar and magazines are piled around the room. The gardens are idyllic, and surround a small swimming-pool.

The highlight of our inspectors' stay was José's outstanding cooking, served in the delightful dining-room – 'the kind of meal you hope to get in a top Parisian restaurant'.

Nearby Castell de Ferro (10 km); Granada, Sierra Nevada and Costa del Sol, all within driving distance.

Plaza Constitución 9 & 10, 18614, Gualchos, Granada
Tel (958) 656034
Location on village square, 10 km up winding road from Castell de Ferro; with garden and car parking on square
Meals breakfast, lunch, dinner
Prices DB&B 9,200pts
Rooms 8 double, one single; all with bath; all rooms have central heating
Facilities dining-room, sitting-room, bar; swimming-pool
Credit cards MC, V
Children not accepted under 12 years
Disabled no special facilities
Pets accepted in bedrooms and garden
Closed Jan and Feb; restaurant only Mon
Proprietor José Gonzalez-Zubiaurre and William Job

Almería

PN Reyes Católicos

Stepping up a gentle hillside just across the road from the beach, this modern Parador, built in the local cubist style which has made Mojácar famous, has a more intimate feel to it than its total of 98 rooms would suggest. Hence its inclusion here, despite exceeding our normal size limits.

In the heart of the complex there is plenty of public space, including an open-plan lounge with a choice of comfortable sitting areas. The whole place is sensitively lit, making the most of natural light. Outside there is an extensive terrace with an inviting swimming-pool.

All the rooms are spacious and spread out – which means that you may have to walk down long corridors. They are almost like holiday apartments and are decorated in a discreet rustic style. Their large bathrooms have double wash-basins and enormous mirrors. All the rooms have balconies and sea views and are well-heated and air-conditioned.

The buffet breakfast lays on everything you could dream of, from cornflakes to *churros* (batter fingers, ideal for dunking). Stay away if you are on a diet.

Nearby Mojácar (1 km); quieter beaches towards Carboneras (22 km); Spaghetti western sets at Mini Hollywood (65 km).

Playa, 04638, Mojácar, Almería
Tel (951) 478250
Location by beach, on main road past Mojácar; with garden and car parking
Meals breakfast, lunch, dinner
Prices rooms 8,000-10,500pts; breakfast 1,100pts; dinner 3,200pts
Rooms 89 double, 9 single; all with bath; all rooms have central heating, air-conditioning, phone, TV, minibar
Facilities dining-room, sitting-room, bar, terrace; tennis court, swimming-pool
Credit cards AE, DC, MC, V
Children welcome
Disabled easy access; ground-floor rooms
Pets not accepted
Closed never
Manager Jesus Cardenas Izquierdo

Cádiz

Town house Parador, Arcos de la Frontera

PN Casa del Corregidor

The winding one-way steets of Arcos bring you steeply uphill to one of Spain's most popular Paradores, the House of the Magistrate. Rebuilt in 1966, it is a fine, white mansion forming one side of the main plaza, overlooking the Guadalete river.

Extensive renovations in 1985 gave the hotel a smart new look; flower-patterned tiles border the white walls along the corridors, tile-pictures tell the stories of bullfights, and potted plants fill the pebbled internal courtyard. Both the bar and the dining-room have French windows opening on to large sunny terraces – perfect places for an evening drink as the sun sinks over the plains. The bedrooms are striking, with dark wooden furniture and red bedspreads; all the rooms we saw had views – either on to the square and the lovely 16thC church of Santa Maria, or over the cliff edge to the patchwork of fields and fruit orchards below. Rooms on this side have sizeable balconies screened off from each other.

The menu includes various specialities cooked and served with sherry from the Jerez *bodegas*; our inspector's meal was good but somewhat spoiled by surly staff – an everyday Parador hazard.
Nearby the churches of Santa Maria and San Pedro, castle; Jerez, Cádiz, Ronda within driving distance.

Plaza de España, 11630, Arcos de la Frontera, Cádiz
Tel (956) 700500
Location on main square, next to Santa Maria (follow Parador signs); with car parking in square
Meals breakfast, lunch, dinner
Prices rooms 11,000-13,000pts; breakfast 1,100pts, dinner 3,200pts
Rooms 20 double, 4 single, all with bath; all rooms have central heating, air-conditioning, phone, TV, minibar, radio
Facilities dining-room, 2 sitting-rooms, bar, 2 terraces
Credit cards AE, DC, MC, V
Children accepted
Disabled lift/elevator
Pets not accepted
Closed never
Manager Salvador Embiz Fabregas

Cádiz

Converted convent, Arcos de la Frontera

El Convento

Although the Roldán family were just sitting down to lunch when we arrived to inspect their pride and joy, they could not have been more welcoming or generous with their time.

José Antonio set up this enchanting hotel-restaurant in 1987, and in 1990 added four new bedrooms to the original four. The new rooms enjoy better panoramic views than from the Parador next door, and for half the price. The original rooms also have balconies and views, and are comfortable, although a little small. They are all decorated with oil paintings by two local artists, Frechilla and Lozano.

The house is full of pictures, pots, and ornaments – especially the main dining-room, which is crammed with delightful objects including pots of fresh honey. The tiny convent chapel is a small second dining-room. There is no sitting-room; but two sun terraces look on to bougainvillaea-clad walls and over the valley. The family's cooking is wholesome and satisfying – menus change daily, and a typical meal might be garlic soup, grilled loin of pork and strawberries with oranges.

We count this place among our favourites and it is a great base for exploring one of Andalucía's most famous 'white towns'.
Nearby churches of Santa Maria and San Pedro, castle.

Calle Maldonado 2, 11630, Arcos de la Frontera, Cádiz
Tel (956) 702333
Location on a tiny back street, past church and Parador; car parking in main square
Meals breakfast, lunch, dinner
Prices rooms 5,000-7,000pts; breakfast 500pts, dinner 2,500-3,000pts
Rooms 6 double, 2 single, all with bath; all rooms have central heating, phone

Facilities 2 dining-rooms, bar, 2 terraces
Credit cards AE, MC, V
Children welcome
Disabled no special facilities
Pets not accepted
Closed never
Proprietor Maria Moreno Moreno

Cádiz

Town hotel, Arcos de la Frontera

Hotel Los Olivos

The receptionist at the Olivos told us (in good English) that the hotel is usually full; it is easy to see why. It is an attractive place, even from the outside – built in typical Arcos style with white-washed walls, yellow tiled roofs and iron grills over the windows, and equipped with pots of geraniums on arched balconies. But it is the interior that really captivates.

The rooms are built around an internal courtyard; café- style tables and chairs are set out in the middle, under palm trees. The breakfast room is decorated in the same dark green furniture and doubles up as a bar; it looks on to a tiny patio containing an old stone well. Behind the glass arches surrounding the courtyard are cosy alcoves of wicker sofas and armchairs, and bowls of fresh flowers.

The bedrooms are light and airy – comfortable, but not cluttered with furniture. All have different cane bedsteads, pale covers and curtains, and mats covering stone-tiled floors. The two front bedrooms have balconies with sweeping views over the plains and the nearby olive-groves from which the hotel takes its name.

Nearby churches of Santa Maria and San Pedro, castle; Jerez, Cádiz, Ronda within driving distance.

San Miguel 2, 11630, Arcos de la Frontera, Cádiz
Tel (956) 700811
Location on road up to Parador, overlooking Guadalete plains; car parking on street
Meals breakfast
Prices rooms 6,050-7,700pts; breakfast 500pts
Rooms 17 double, 2 single; all with bath; all rooms have central heating, air-conditioning, phone, TV, minibar, radio
Facilities sitting-rooms, TV room, bar/breakfast room
Credit cards AE, MC, V
Children welcome
Disabled lift/elevator
Pets not accepted
Closed never
Proprietor Manuel Armario Dormido

Cádiz

Converted convent, Vejer de la Frontera

Convento de San Francisco

Vejer is a delightful medieval town crowning a solitary hill near the coast. In the old part of town, the Felipe brothers have lovingly converted a 17thC convent into an unusual hotel; a set of photographs in the echoing *taberna* tell the story of the renovations. Many of the remains have been preserved – a Roman mosaic in the hall, a cabinet of medieval pottery on the stairs, the old choir stalls and frescos in the sitting-room. The bedrooms still have their original stone arches visible in the walls and the furniture has been designed in harmony – arched bed-heads, stripped pine desks, wooden shutters. The result is effective – the simplicity of a nun's cell with the facilities of a modern hotel.

The refectory still serves as a dining-room, still with wooden benches and tables lining the walls. Bright modern cushions and abstract modern paintings add a splash of colour. Our inspector's meal, the *menu del dia*, was excellent, piping hot and served by cheerful staff. Outside the dining-room is an obscure metal sculpture, two floors high. The centre-piece of the Convento is the 'choir hall' – a great place to sit when the sun filters through the windows in the early morning.

Nearby Castle, churches, Jewish Quarter.

La Plazuela, 11150, Vejer de la Frontera, Cádiz
Tel (956) 451001
Location on small square in old part of town, round corner from main street on cliff edge; car parking on main street
Meals breakfast, lunch, dinner
Prices rooms 8,000-10,000pts; breakfast 800pts, menu 3,000pts
Rooms 22 double, 1 single, one family room; all with bath; all rooms have phone
Facilities dining-room, sitting-room, cafeteria, bar
Credit cards MC, V
Children welcome
Disabled lift/elevator
Pets not accepted
Closed never
Manager Juan Pablo Felipe Tablado

Cádiz

Hotel Brasilia

This white colonial-style building is conveniently situated for both beach and town. The bedrooms and public rooms are modern and spacious, and walls are decorated with wonderful Manrique water-colours of Spanish scenes. One of the Brasilia's key features is the green and white conservatory which looks out on to an enticing swimming-pool and tiled sun terrace – an excellent alternative to a crowded beach in high season. If you fancy a few days of luxury after tearing around Andalucía, this is a great place to relax.

Nearby beach (200 m); Sanlúcar de Barrameda (10 km); *manzanilla* sherry, Jerez (30 km).

Avenida del Faro 12, 11550, Chipiona, Cádiz
Tel (956) 371054
Location on quiet street, 200m from sea-front; with car parking on street
Meals breakfast, lunch, dinner
Prices rooms (1991) 4,700-6,400pts; breakfast 500pts, dinner 1,200pts
Rooms 42 double, 2 single; all with bath; all rooms have central heating, air-conditioning, phone, radio; some rooms have TV
Facilities dining-room, sitting-room, cafeteria, terrace
Credit cards AE, DC, V
Children accepted
Disabled ground-floor rooms
Pets not accepted
Closed never; restaurant only in winter
Manager Juan Gonzalez del

Hotel Capele

The grey concrete balconies of the Hotel Capele, squeezed between town houses in the old part of Jerez, are enough to put you off staying there. But venture inside and you will be amazed by the smart public rooms, cool marble corridors and elegant bedrooms. Our inspectors were particularly impressed by the reproduction antique furniture in their room and the large chequered bathroom. There is a welcoming traditional-style dining-room – with stone arches, wooden wine racks and beamed ceilings. Definitely the best choice for a night in Jerez.

Nearby sherry bodegas, horse fairs; Sanlúcar de Barrameda (30 km); Cádiz (35 km).

Corredera 58, 11402, Jerez de la Frontera, Cádiz
Tel (956) 346400
Location on main square; car parking on street
Meals breakfast, lunch, dinner
Prices rooms 9,600-14,700pts; breakfast 600pts, dinner 2,500pts
Rooms 43 double, 12 single; all with bath; all rooms have central heating, air-conditioning, phone; most rooms have TV
Facilities dining-room, sitting-room/bar
Credit cards AE, DC, V
Children accepted
Disabled no special facilities
Pets not accepted
Closed never
Manager Marta Jimenez Marchena

Cádiz

Converted convent, La Almoraima

Casa Convento

Opposite a large factory on the main road to Jimena, a small sign points up a wooded drive to the Casa Convento. Following the road, you pass from scrubby trees dotted with nesting boxes to beautiful landscaped gardens, and end up in front of the yellow and white faade of a 17thC convent. Tall palm trees shade the arched windows and elegant pillars along the front of the building. The place is serene – it comes as quite a surprise to discover that until recently it was a hunting lodge (witness the mounted hunting trophies in the public rooms).

Despite its grandiose appearance, the hotel is surprisingly informal and relaxed; the public rooms are obviously used, not just admired. The 'bar' consists of a trolley of spirits, the 'games room' a billiard table, the 'music room' a mini grand piano, and the 'library' a couple of ancient book shelves. The rooms upstairs are reminiscent of an English country house – with tapestries on the sitting-room walls and chandeliers over the long dining-room table. Bedrooms are comfortable, overlooking either the gardens or the central courtyard. The chapel and the old bell-towers are the only reminders that this was once a convent.

Nearby Castellar de la Frontera; Algeciras (25 km).

La Almoraima, 11350, Castellar de la Frontera, Cádiz
Tel (956) 693002
Location in wooded grounds, 12 km north of Algeciras on N340; with gardens and car parking
Meals breakfast, lunch, dinner
Prices rooms 7,000-14,000pts; breakfast 500pts, dinner 2,500pts
Rooms 7 double, 4 single; all with bath; all rooms have central heating, phone; most rooms have fires, some rooms have TV
Facilities dining-room, sitting-room, games room; swimming-pool, tennis court, mini-golf, horse riding
Credit cards AE, MC, V
Children not accepted
Disabled access difficult
Pets accepted in bedrooms
Closed never
Manager Juan Montoya

Cádiz

Town house, Sanlúcar de Barrameda

Posada de Palacio

Antonio and Renata Navarrete set up this pension in 1986, when they moved from Switzerland. It is a typical Andalucian town house, near the Bombadilla sherry bodegas in the old part of the town. If you get lost, follow your nose; an overpowering smell of Sanlúcar's famous manzanilla lingers around the warehouses.

The guest-house is built around a courtyard of original stone floor-tiles. Most of the bedrooms are in this part of the building, including two ground-floor suites. All the rooms are unconventional, adding to their charm. Some could benefit from refurbishment, but all are clean and comfortable, and those we saw were very spacious – we had a cavernous bathroom, even bigger than our bedroom. Another is the superb home-made breakfast, which we ate in our room overlooking the tiny garden.

The public rooms are full of interesting objects that the couple have collected over the years; an old grinding wheel hangs next to modern film posters in the bar, miniature pictures decorate the walls, and fresh flowers abound. You are constantly reminded that this is a home as well as a hotel. Tables are set outside under the wisteria, and up ivy-covered steps, four new rooms look on to a large stone sun-terrace.

Nearby Castle, palace, sherry bodegas, beach.

Calle Caballeros 11, 11540, Sanlúcar de Barrameda, Cádiz
Tel (956) 364840
Location near castle and palace, in old part of town; car parking on street
Meals breakfast
Prices rooms 4,500-8,000pts; breakfast 500pts
Rooms 11 double, all with bath; all rooms have phone
Facilities sitting-room, TV room, bar/breakfast room, terrace
Credit cards DC, MC, V
Children welcome
Disabled ground-floor rooms
Pets not accepted
Closed Jan and Feb
Proprietor Antonio and Renata Navarrete

Cádiz

Hilltop hotel, Grazalema

Hostal Grazalema

Nestling in the mountains of the Sierra de Zafalgar is the tiny 'white town' of Grazalema, one of the prettiest and most unspoiled in Andalucía. Its only hotel is on the edge of the town, looking down the valley from a rocky outcrop. The low white building is in fact modern, but its yellow-tiled roofs and whitewashed walls blend in perfectly with the traditional shuttered houses that line the two main streets. The spectacular views from the hotel's terraces – mile upon mile of olive and pine groves, meadows of flowers and towering mountains (all part of a National Park) – never fail to bring whoops of joy from newly arrived visitors.

The interior is mainly open-plan, with a reception area, bar and sitting-room on one level and a pretty red and white dining-room on a lower level. Striped hand-woven rugs and curtains, made on old wooden looms in the village, brighten up white walls, and wrought-iron lamps hang throughout. Arched French windows open on to the lawns and swimming-pool area – a children's paradise. Most of the bedrooms have balconies facing this way; the ones we saw were spacious, clean and comfortable with traditional local trappings.

Nearby Other 'white towns' (Ubrique, Ronda, Arcos).

11610, Grazalema, Cádiz
Tel (956) 132136
Location on hill on edge of village; with garden and car parking
Meals breakfast, lunch, dinner
Prices rooms 4,030-5,940pts; breakfast 475pts; meals 1,875pts
Rooms 24 double, all with bath; all rooms have central heating, phone
Facilities dining-room, sitting-room, TV room, terrace; swimming-pool
Credit cards V
Children accepted
Disabled no special facilities
Pets not accepted
Closed never
Manager Rodrigo Valle Naranjo

Málaga

Area introduction

Hotels on the Costa del Sol

'Charming' and 'small' are not the first adjectives that spring to mind when considering hotels along the Costa del Sol. It has taken some searching to find such places along this 200 km holiday playground, and many of the hotels we describe in detail are not actually on the coast, but behind it, hidden away in the mountains. Anyone who wants to be on the coast itself might consider some of the hotels listed below. A word of warning: most of them get very booked up in high season, so plan well in advance.

Tarifa (an unspoiled fishing village 22 km south-west of Algeciras) is not technically part of the Costa del Sol, but the 20-room Dos Mares (Tel (956) 684035), a comfortable Dutch-run inn right on the beach, definitely deserves a mention. It is close enough for a day trip to 'Gib' to see the rock, the apes and the British bobbies, but staying overnight here is an expensive business. The pick of Gibraltar's hotels is the Rock (Tel (350) 73000), a large, rather old-fashioned establishment, serving traditional British food.

At the true heart of the Costa del Sol is smart Marbella, the most up-market of the resorts. Hotels on the less crowded beaches just out of town are the best bet, such as Las Chapas (Tel (952) 831375), a self-contained holiday complex with 120 rooms and lots of leisure activities on offer. If you want to splash out, stay at the Puente Romano, an extremely elegant hotel set in luxuriant gardens (Tel (952) 770100).

Further round the coast are the major package holiday resorts of Torremolinos and Fuengirola. The Montemar (Torremolinos) is one of the few hotels of any character; its 40 rooms are built around a typical Andalucían courtyard (Tel (952) 381577). A stone's throw from Torremolinos is Málaga, not just an airport but a sprawling city, best avoided in high season. If you have to stay here, the Palacío – elegant, luxurious, with a roof-top swimming-pool (Tel (952) 215185) – and the Casa Curro – central, comfortable (Tel (952) 227200) – are good alternatives to the Parador. Most hotels run a bus service to the airport.

East of Málaga is the quieter resort of Nerja. The famous view from the Balcón de Europa is definitely worth stopping for, and you could do worse than staying in the pretty but tatty Cala Bella in the heart of town. It is a friendly family-run hotel with a superb terrace where guests dine in summer (Tel (952) 520700).

Beyond the eastern extremity of the Costa del Sol at Almería is a hotel which deserves a mention, the 8-room San José , a very attractive family-run place next to the magnificent natural park of Cabo de Gata (Tel (951) 366974). Service is reportedly friendly, and the atmosphere tranquil; it is high on our agenda for inspection, so we should welcome reports.

Hotel prices

As we explain in the Introduction, many hotels did not know their 1992 prices when we were preparing this edition. It is always wise to check room prices when making a booking or taking a room: hotels sometimes change their prices by much more than inflationary amounts. And Italian hotel prices are particularly likely to change this year.

Málaga

Beach hotel, Nerja

Hostal Avalon

The British are not the only northerners who like the idea of escaping our gloomy weather and setting up shop at Europe's southern extremity; this neat, modern *hostal* is run by a Swedish couple. When we arrived, Christer was whitewashing walls while Britt prepared the evening meal – Spanish meatroll and figs (from the garden) in brandy.

You eat on the covered terrace above the garden or at one end of the open-plan sitting/dining area. At the other end of this airy room are comfortable sofas next to a bookshelf of well-thumbed novels, and opposite is a smart modern bar. Public space may be limited when the hotel is full, but there is always the garden or the large, red-brick roof terrace (if you are feeling too lazy to cross the road to the beach). All but one of the bedrooms have balconies with sea views; they are decorated in pastel shades, and are clean and comfortable.

This is the kind of place you can treat like home; there is even a well-equipped kitchen for guests staying more than a week. The only reservation we have is that the *hostal* is built above the busy coast road. But the Avalon's fabulous views of the sea and mountains make up for the dull murmur of traffic.

Nearby beach; Nerja (2 km), Málaga (47 km).

Punta Lara, 29780, Nerja, Málaga
Tel (952) 520698
Location on main road from Nerja to Málaga, 2 km from town; with garden and shaded car parking in drive
Meals breakfast, dinner
Prices rooms 3,500-6,500pts; breakfast 450pts, lunch 1,500, dinner 2,500pts
Rooms 8 double, 5 with shower, 3 with bath; extra beds available; all rooms have electric heaters
Facilities dining-room/ sitting-room/bar, 2 terraces
Credit cards not accepted
Children welcome; but not safe for small children
Disabled one ground-floor room
Pets welcome
Closed Nov to Feb
Proprietor Britt Johansson and Christer Fagerlund

Málaga

Hotel Miami

Somewhere in the ocean of concrete formed by the merger of Málaga and Torremolinos, a small sign directs you off the main coast road to the Miami. It is set in its own rounded driveway and is completely walled off from its surroundings – it feels just like an island. The house was built by Picasso's cousin as a holiday villa and has made an unusual hotel, set around a lagoon-like swimming pool. Palms and banana trees overshadow the pool and give it an exotic, tropical feel – you could be in the Caribbean rather than in the heart of Torremolinos, only yards away from a crowded beach and busy sea-front.

Some of the bedrooms are in need of attention; ours was worn and dusty, but adequate. Most have balconies, and all are cool and airy. One of the key features of the hotel is the grotto-like sitting-room, with its mixture of square and round windows peeping out of pebble-dashed walls and its curious fireplace of piled stones. It is full of interesting objects – animal-skin seats, copper pots, pilot lanterns.

There is no restaurant, but the Miami does serve probably the only 'Spanish' breakfast in Torremolinos – on the terrace above the pool.

Nearby beach; Málaga (15 km), Marbella (45 km).

Calle Aladino 14, 29620,
Torremolinos, Málaga
Tel (952) 385255
Location on quiet side-street,
50 m from beach; signed from
main road through
Torremolinos; with garden
and ample car parking in drive
Meals breakfast
Prices rooms 3,113-4,717pts;
breakfast 250pts
Rooms 26 double, all with
bath; all rooms have central
heating, phone
Facilities sitting-room,
bar/patio, swimming-pool
Credit cards not accepted
Children accepted
Disabled 6 ground-floor rooms
Pets accepted
Closed never
Manager Mercedes Gomez
Delgado

Málaga

Modern Parador, Antequera

PN de Antequera

Although it is large and modern, this was one of our favourite Paradors, with exceptionally welcoming and helpful staff (so often the Parador weakness). It is set on a hill, overlooking plains and mountains and the pretty white town of Antequera. The two wings of the white building look on to a magnificent swimming-pool, surrounded by lawns and shady trees. Most bedrooms face this way, and have either direct access to the gardens or balconies overlooking them. The rooms are large, cool and comfortable, and have the most powerful showers in Spain.

The dining-room and split-level sitting-room are reminiscent of an Alpine chalet – add snow to the craggy mountain tops seen through the large windows, and you could be in Switzerland. The food, however, is definitely Spanish – delicious shellfish, local trout, paella, almond tarts. All the public rooms are large and formal; sofas, rocking-chairs and card tables are set out as if they were on display, not in use. Yet the atmosphere in the rest of the Parador is relaxed and informal, and it makes an excellent base for exploring the surrounding countryside and the fascinating prehistoric monuments in the town.

Nearby dolmens – prehistoric funerary chambers; Roman remains, castle; Costa del Sol (50 km); Granada (100 km).

Paseo García del Olmo, 29200, Antequera, Málaga
Tel (952) 840261
Location on hill on edge of town; with gardens and car parking
Meals breakfast, lunch, dinner
Prices rooms 8,000-10,000pts, breakfast 1,100pts, dinner 3,200pts
Rooms 55 double, all with bath; all rooms have central heating, air-conditioning, phone, TV, minibar
Facilities dining-room, 2 sitting-rooms, bar; swimming-pool
Credit cards AE, DC, MC, V
Children welcome
Disabled ground-floor rooms
Pets not accepted
Closed never
Manager Manuel Martinez Martinez

Málaga

Hilltop Parador, Málaga

PN de Gibralfaro

If you have time to spare in Málaga, spend it at this Parador, set in the peaceful gardens of the Gibralfaro on a hilltop above the city. It is the setting and the spectacular views, rather than the hotel itself, that make the Parador an exceptional place to stay in this drab concrete port. The approach road winds through pine and eucalyptus trees, ending up at an stone-arcaded building, just below the remains of the Phoenician/Moorish castle. Although it has only 12 rooms for guests, the Parador is often thronged with people who come up here to escape the heat and hassle, and to enjoy the views of the port and Costa del Sol while they dine on the terraces.

A thoroughly well-run hotel in a position like this would be a real gem. Sadly, we thought that the hotel itself felt rather unloved – worn furniture, bare bedroom walls, formal staff. It has all the usual Parador facilities – spacious bedrooms with large balconies, a busy bar serving excellent snacks, and an attractive dining-room with tables outside under the arches.

Dining up here, with the sea shimmering below you and Gibraltar just visible in the distance, it is hard to believe that you are in the heart of Málaga.

Nearby gardens of Gibralfaro, Alcazaba; Costa del Sol.

Monte de Gibralfaro, 29016, Málaga
Tel (952) 221903
Location on hill above city, next to castle; with gardens and shaded car parking
Meals breakfast, lunch, dinner
Prices rooms 10,000-11,500pts; breakfast 1,100pts, dinner 3,200pts
Rooms 12 double, all with bath; all rooms have central heating, air-conditioning, phone, TV, minibar
Facilities dining-room, sitting-room/bar, terrace
Credit cards AE, DC, MC, V
Children welcome
Disabled easy access to 6 rooms
Pets not accepted
Closed never
Proprietor Joaquin Martin Planelles

Málaga

Old water-mill, Benaoján

Molino del Santo

A short drive (or train-ride) from Ronda is the sleepy village of Benaoján, perched on a herb-scented mountainside, surrounded by olive and almond groves. Its water-mill, beside the bubbling stream below the village, was converted into a hotel in 1987 by a young English couple, Andy Chapell and Pauline Elkin, who fled the rat-race in favour of this idyllic spot. We could see why as soon as we arrived, on a timeless Sunday morning when the guests were eating a leisurely buffet breakfast under the willow trees on the stone terrace. Dinner is also served out here in the summer (a delicious-sounding set menu with plenty of choice and vegetarian options). To the amusement of the locals, guests also get a real English tea with home-made cakes.

Inside, the rooms are comfortable and home-like; the sitting-room still has some of its original trappings – an oak-beamed ceiling and old grinding stones. The bedrooms vary in size (some take extra beds) and are simply furnished, with bright locally made rugs. Six have small terraces overlooking a beautiful swimming-pool, shaded by willow, fig and quince trees.

Andy and Pauline rent out mountain bikes for exploring and run excursions to all the local sights.

Nearby cave of La Pileta – paleolithic art; white towns.

Bda Estación, 29370, Benaoján, Málaga
Tel (952) 167151
Location by river in village, near railway station; with gardens and shaded car parking
Meals breakfast, lunch, tea, dinner
Prices B&B 3,500-7,000pts; lunch 400-600pts, dinner 2,000pts; children's meals available

Rooms 6 double, 3 family rooms; all with shower; all rooms have electric heaters, phone, tea and coffee facilities
Facilities dining-room, sitting-room, bar, terrace; pool
Credit cards MC, V
Children welcome
Disabled access difficult
Pets not normally accepted
Closed possibly in winter
Proprietor Andy Chapell and Pauline Elkin

Málaga

Hunting lodge, Ojén

Refugio de Juanar

Parador signs still point the way from Ojén to the Refugio in the wild foothills of the Sierra Blanca, although it ceased to be a Parador several years ago. Now run (at least as efficiently as it ever was) by the local authorities, it has become a popular mountain retreat from the pressure of the Costa del Sol – for locals and tourists alike.

It was built as a hunting lodge at the turn of the century and still retains its 'hunting' atmosphere. The sitting-room is an informal jumble of leather sofas around a log fire – deer antlers and zebra skin hang among old English hunting scenes on the walls. Photographs in the bar show wildlife from around the Refugio – ibex and peacocks on the lawns, birds of prey in action. The bedrooms are comfortably rustic and smell of wood-smoke. The restaurant continues on the hunting theme, specializing in game casseroles and local produce. It opens out on to a terrace overlooking pine trees.

Apart from the neat swimming-pool and tennis court, the grounds are wonderfully wild – the perfect place for children of an appropriate age to go exploring. No one with a taste for the outdoors is likely to get bored here.

Nearby National Reserve; Ojén (10 km); Marbella (20 km).

Sierra Blanca, 29610, Ojén, Málaga
Tel (952) 881000
Location in mountains, 10 km from Ojen; follow signs to Refugio; with grounds and car parking in drive
Meals breakfast, lunch, dinner
Prices rooms 5,450-7,600pts; breakfast 700pts, dinner 2,450pts
Rooms 20 double, one single, 4 family rooms; all with bath; all rooms have central heating, phone, minibar; most rooms have TV
Facilities dining-room, sitting-room, TV room, bar; swimming-pool, tennis court, table tennis
Credit cards AE, DC, MC, V
Children accepted
Disabled some ground-floor rooms **Pets** not accepted
Closed never
Manager José Gómez Avila

Málaga

Country inn, Alhaurín el Grande

Finca La Mota

Behind a high white wall in the lush countryside outside the village of Alhaurín lies this three-hundred-year-old farmhouse, now run as a friendly country inn by a British/American combination, Jean and Arun Narang. The hotel's six-acre lawns and shady trees surround a swimming-pool, but for those wanting sand and sea, the Costa del Sol is only a short drive away through the mountains. Most guests prefer the peace of the Andalucian countryside, and enjoy the beautiful walks or rides (on the family ponies) in the surrounding hills.

The rooms surround an attractive central patio, in typical Andalucian style. They are pleasantly rustic, with open fires for cold winter days and a mixture of English and Andalucian antiques, collected by the Narangs over the years. Some of the seven bedrooms have four-poster beds, and all are bright and comfortable. Extra beds are available.

The Narangs' restaurant is very popular, offering interesting dishes that are far from the Spanish norm (including Indian and Malaysian curries) and plenty of fresh vegetables from the garden. They are happy to cook guests' special requests and have a big barbecue every weekend.

Nearby Coín (10 km); Málaga (25 km).

Partido Urique, 29100, Alhaurín El Grande, Málaga
Tel (952)594120/490901
Location in agricultural countryside about 2 km SW on mijas road out of Alhaurin; with garden and car parking
Meals breakfast, lunch, dinner
Prices rooms 4,000-8,000pts with English breakfast
Rooms 6 double, 3 with bath; one family room with bath; all rooms have tea/coffee kit and electric heaters; some rooms have TV
Facilities dining-room, sitting-room, bar, terrace; swimming-pool
Credit cards AE, MC, V
Children welcome
Disabled 3 ground-floor rooms
Pets accepted
Closed never
Proprietors Arun and Jean Narang

Mallorca

Hotels on the Balearic Islands

The *Islas Baleares* consist of four islands. Largest and most well-known is Mallorca, a popular holiday destination comprising beautiful sandy beaches in the south, and towering mountains, sheer cliffs and rocky coves in the north. One of the island's smartest hotels is on its northernmost point, the Cap de Formentor – the luxurious 130-room Formentor (Tel (971) 531300), splendidly set amidst pine trees on the edge of a beach. It has excellent facilities, especially for children, and comfortable rooms with perfect views of sea and peaks. Deia, close to the rugged north-west coast, has two smart hotels of note; La Residencia (page 175) and the Es Molí, which is stunningly situated on the edge of the cliff but lacks the personal touches of La Residencia. The rooms have recently been redecorated and the gardens are luxurious, 'a dazzling array of trailing flowers, laden fruit trees and immaculate lawns, lovingly tended by an army of gardeners'. For those who want to stay nearer Palma, the 60-room Punta Negra (recently taken over by Trusthouse Forte) is in a fabulous position on the Costa de Bendinat, away from the hordes but still reasonably convenient. Further away along the south coast, a simple but popular hotel is the Cala Santanyi in the village of the same name. The building is a white arc so that all rooms have a view of one of the most perfect bays imaginable (Tel (971) 653200). Further round the coast is the white holiday complex of Cala d'Or.

Menorca, the smaller neighbour of Mallorca, is a different kettle of fish. Unlike Mallorca, it has escaped mass hotel-building and is still a quiet family holiday island with numerous unspoilt beaches. Of the few hotels, the 75-room Port Mahón is a comfortable, old-fashioned place overlooking the Mahón harbour, praised for its excellent friendly service (Tel (971) 362600); the Rocamar at nearby Cala Fonduco is a restaurant with rooms, providing some of the best seafood on the island and good-value accommodation (Tel (971) 365601).

Ibiza, smaller though more touristy than Menorca, has a Moorish feel to it – the last vestiges of its 8thC occupation. One of the island's few luxury hotels is the Hacienda, situated 22 km from the main town; it has 65 comfortable rooms in traditional white houses. The setting is lovely and the facilities are extensive (Tel (971) 333046).

Formentera is a tiny island off the south coast of Ibiza. History and tourism have left it virtually untouched, and it has endless deserted beaches served by a handful of hotels. The choice is mainly between small and simple, such as the 20-room Sa Volta at Es Pujols (Tel (971) 328125), and big and smart, such as the 330-room La Mola at Es Arenals (Tel (971) 328069).

Taking pets abroad
Although our fact boxes state whether pets are accepted by hotels, residents of Britain should be aware that they should not be tempted to take theirs abroad. The difficulty arises when returning to Britain: because of the risk of bringing an animal infected with rabies, most animals would have to go into a long period of quarantine.

Mallorca

Village hotel, Bañalbufar

Hotel Mar i Vent

The Mar i Vent is not a luxury hotel; but what it lacks in refinement, it makes up for in friendly atmosphere and indisputable charm. Tony and Juana Vives, a delightful brother-and-sister team, treat their guests like old friends; many return year after year, and it is easy to see why.

The hotel is perched on the side of a terraced hill that plunges dramatically down to a rocky cove on Mallorca's spectacular west coast. The views are unbeatable; our inspector enjoyed a mesmerising sunset over the sea from her first-floor balcony. Half the bedrooms are in the main building, the others in a similar tall white building next door. Far from being second-rate (as many annexe rooms are), these are in fact larger and smarter than the original rooms, and have the added bonus of being out of ear-shot of the swimming-pool (a very lively place on a hot day). All public rooms are in the main hotel – a comfortable sitting-room upstairs and a cool spartan one downstairs, a pretty L-shaped dining-room and a large terrace (with excruciatingly uncomfortable iron chairs).

There is little choice for dinner, which can at best be described as tasty home-cooking.

Nearby Valldemosa (15 km), Esporles (15 km).

Mayor 49, 07191, Bañalbufar, Mallorca
Tel (971) 618000
Location on seaward side of road, on edge of village; with garden and car parking
Meals breakfast, dinner; lunch instead of dinner on Sun
Prices rooms 4,200-5,250pts; breakfast 600pts, dinner 1,800pts
Rooms 16 double, 2 single, 2 family rooms, all with bath; all rooms have central heating, phone
Facilities bar, dining-room, 2 sitting-rooms, terraces; swimming-pool, tennis court
Credit cards not accepted
Children welcome; mini swimming-pool
Disabled no special facilities
Pets not accepted in public rooms **Closed** Dec and Jan
Proprietor Antonio and Juana Vives Alberti

Mallorca

Country hotel, Deia

Hotel La Residencia

Almost everything about the Residencia is out of the ordinary. Set above the road at the north end of the fashionable village of Deia, it is a cluster of creeper-covered stone buildings in beautiful tiered gardens. The core of the hotel is a 16thC manor house; its original olive mill is now the restaurant. There is also an annexe above the swimming-pool behind the main hotel, built in the same pink stone with white shutters.

The interior of the hotel is exquisitely furnished with antique pieces, colourful rugs and fascinating modern art (from the private collection of the hotel's German owner). Bedrooms vary in size – from an almost poky single to an enormous suite in a separate building. All have lovely wooden furniture and many have antique or four-poster beds. There are bars and breakfast-rooms in both parts of the hotel, though most people eat out on the terraces overlooking either the swimming-pool (surrounded by elegant cypresses and silver birches) or the front lawns.

Another highlight is the hotel's acclaimed restaurant, El Olivo. Its lofty ceiling, dripping candelabra, cane furniture and elegant tables, set among relics of the olive mill, make a wonderfully romantic setting for an excellent four- or eight-course dinner.

Nearby Valldemosa (15 km), Sóller (15 km).

07179, Deia, Mallorca
Tel (971) 639011
Location at N end of village, signed from road as 'El Olivo'; with garden and car parking
Meals breakfast, lunch, dinner
Prices rooms 16,000-32,500pts with breakfast; meals 3,500-4,000pts
Rooms 25 double, 10 single, 14 suites, all with bath; all rooms have central heating, air-conditioning, phone,

hair-drier
Facilities restaurant, 4 sitting-rooms, 4 bars; swimming-pool, tennis court, private cove
Credit cards AE, DC, MC, V
Children welcome
Disabled no special facilities
Pets small dogs accepted
Closed Jan and Feb; restaurant only, Wed
Managers William Schuler and Talis Waldren

Mallorca

Town hotel, Cala Ratjada

Hotel Ses Rotges

Ten or 15 years ago it might have been a surprise to find a well-established French-run hotel in the middle of this village on Mallorca's east coast. Today it would come as no surprise at all – Cala Ratjada is now a lively cosmopolitan holiday town. The Tétards have kept pace with the local development, cleverly extending their pink-stone hotel in the same style as the original buildings, with arched windows and wrought iron balconies.

The hotel, on the corner of two quiet streets near the beach, overlooks a quiet internal courtyard – a wonderful place to relax among trailing plants, overhanging bougainvillaea and a profusion of colourful flowers. The popular restaurant adjoins the courtyard and is set with red and white tables under a beamed roof. In winter, dinner is served inside in another large, cheerful room. The oldest part of the building, around the original chimney, is now a cosy sitting-room. The bedrooms are spacious and airy; they are supposed to be 'individually furnished', but the ones we saw all had the same tiled floors, wooden furniture and bedheads, star-shaped mirrors and modern bathrooms.

Food is a highlight, earning one of the island's very few Michelin stars.

Nearby Artà (10 km); Manacor (30 km).

Rafael Blanes 21, 07590, Cala Ratjada, Mallorca
Tel (971) 563108
Location in quiet street 200m from beach; with car parking in street
Meals breakfast, lunch, dinner
Prices rooms 7,500pts; breakfast 950pts, meals 2,500pts
Rooms 24 double, all with bath; all rooms have central heating, air-conditioning, phone
Facilities bar, dining-room, sitting-room, TV room, patio
Credit cards AE, DC, MC, V
Children tolerated
Disabled access generally difficult; one ground-floor room
Pets not accepted
Closed 1 Nov to 1 Apr
Proprietor Gérard Charles Tetard

Mallorca

Country hotel, Valldemosa

Vistamar de Valldemosa

Vistamar is an appropriate name for this lovely old villa set in countryside on rocky cliffs – you get tantalizing glimpses of the sea through the tangle of pines and olives in front of the hotel. Paths go some way down the cliffs; you cannot get right down to the cove from here, but then you don't really need to – the hotel has its own spectacularly positioned swimming-pool, and is only minutes away from the delightful port of Valldemosa.

A stone archway leads under a balustraded balcony (impressively lit at night) into a cobbled courtyard, with the rooms of the hotel set around three sides. The atmosphere inside is of absolute calm. Rooms are beamed and have heavy wooden doors and antique furniture. Comfortable green and white sofas and chairs are dotted around the two white-walled sitting-rooms, and interesting modern art adds a splash of colour. Dinner is served either inside, or in the partly glassed-in terrace overlooking the gardens.

Bedrooms, some of which have large sun terraces, are cool and comfortable, with spotless white bathrooms, linen bedcovers and massive wooden cupboards. There are further examples of modern art along the walls of the tall corridors.

Nearby Valldemosa; Bañalbufar (15 km); Deia (15 km).

07170, Valldemosa, Mallorca
Tel (971) 612300
Location on flat olive plain, 2.5km W of Valldemosa; with garden and car parking
Meals breakfast, lunch, dinner
Prices rooms 15,900-21,200pts with breakfast; breakfast 1,275,meals 2,000pts
Rooms 9 double, all with bath; all rooms have central heating, phone, TV, minibar; a few rooms have jacuzzi

Facilities dining-rooms, sitting-rooms, bar, terrace; swimming-pool
Credit cards AE, MC, V
Children accepted
Disabled access difficult
Pets not accepted
Closed Nov and 2 weeks in Dec
Proprietor Pedro Coll Pastor

Mallorca

Hotel L'Hermitage

The great attraction of L'Hermitage is its setting – tucked away in a beautiful fruit-growing valley in the mountains, miles from the beaten track (no mean achievement in Mallorca). It consists of a somewhat strange selection of buildings: a narrow 17thC stone manor house (with tower), a two-storey modern block overlooking an orchard and a totally separate cloister with 16 twisted stone pillars enclosing lemon and orange trees. Only four of the bedrooms are in the old house. These have tiny windows peering out of thick walls, making the rooms beautifully cool but also very dim; with polished furniture on old tiled floors, they have much more character than the modern rooms – though these are also cool and comfortable, with palatial bathrooms.

There is a warren of tiny public rooms in the old part of the hotel, including an elegant downstairs sitting-room and a cosy upstairs one with an open fire. In contrast, the dining-room in the old olive mill is enormous. It still has a sloping, beamed ceiling and the original grinding-stones, which make an admirable table for the generous buffet breakfasts. Outside, there is a terrace lined with tables, a swimming-pool among the pine trees and two tennis courts are found on the far side of the orchards.
Nearby Buñola (10 km), Alaró (10 km).

07110, Orient, Mallorca
Tel (971) 613300
Location in fruit-orchard valley in mountains, 1km E of Orient; with garden and car parking
Meals breakfast, lunch, dinner
Prices rooms 13,000-20,000pts with breakfast; meals about 3,000pts
Rooms 20 double, all with bath; all rooms have phone, minibar; some rooms have central heating, TV
Facilities dining-room, 2 sitting-rooms, bar, terrace; sauna, tennis court, swimming-pool
Credit cards AE, DC, MC, V
Children accepted
Disabled no special facilities
Pets not accepted
Closed 1 Nov to 15 Dec
Manager Ismal Grande

Index of hotel names

Hotels are arranged in order of the most distinctive part of their name; other parts of the name are also given, except that very common prefixes such as 'Hotel' and 'La' are omitted. The abbreviation PN is used for Parador Nacional (see Introduction for further explanation). Hotels covered in the several Area introductions, and in the feature boxes on Paradores, are not indexed.

A

B

C

Index of hotel names

Index of hotel names

Index of hotel names

Index of hotel names

Index of hotel names

Index of hotel locations

In this index, hotels are arranged by the name of the city, town or village they are in or near. Where a hotel is located in a very small place, it may be indexed under a nearby place which is more easily found on maps. The abbreviation PN is used for Parador Nacional (see Introduction for further explanation).

A

B

Index of hotel locations

Index of hotel locations

Index of hotel locations

Index of hotel locations

Index of hotel locations